Douglas Gregory

AGAINST
INTELLECTUAL PROPERTY

"Against Intellectual Property" first appeared as part of the symposium Applications of Libertarian Legal Theory, published in the *Journal of Libertarian Studies* 15, no. 2 (Spring 2001).

Copyright © 2008 Ludwig von Mises Institute

For information, write the Ludwig von Mises Institute, 518 West Magnolia Avenue, Auburn, Alabama 36832, U.S.A

AGAINST INTELLECTUAL PROPERTY

N. Stephan Kinsella

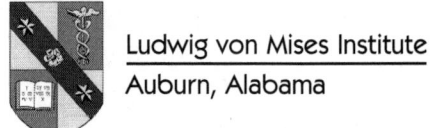
Ludwig von Mises Institute
Auburn, Alabama

CONTENTS

PROPERTY RIGHTS: TANGIBLE AND INTANGIBLE 7

SUMMARY OF IP LAW 9
    Type of IP 9
    Copyright 10
    Patent 10
    Trade Secret 11
    Trademark 12
    IP Rights and Relation to Tangible Property 14

LIBERTARIAN PERSPECTIVES ON IP 16
    The Spectrum 16
    Utilitarian Defenses of IP 19
    Some Problems with Natural Rights 23

IP AND PROPERTY RIGHTS 28
    Property and Scarcity 28
    Scarcity and Ideas 32
    Creation vs. Scarcity 36
    Two Types of Homesteading 43

IP AS CONTRACT 45
  The Limits of Contract......................... 45
  Contract vs. Reserved Rights................... 47
  Copyright and Patent........................... 55
  Trade Secret 56
  Trademark...................................... 58

CONCLUSION 59

APPENDIX
  Some Questionable Examples of Patents and Copyrights .. 60

BIBLIOGRAPHY 63

AGAINST INTELLECTUAL PROPERTY

Property Rights:
Tangible and Intangible

All libertarians favor property rights, and agree that property rights include rights in tangible resources. These resources include immovables (realty) such as land and houses, and movables such as chairs, clubs, cars, and clocks.¹

Further, all libertarians support rights in one's own body. Such rights may be called "self-ownership" as long as one keeps in mind that there is dispute about whether such body-ownership is alienable in the same way that rights in homesteadable, external objects are alienable.² In any

---

¹Terms like "realty," "personalty," and "tangible" are common-law terms; analogous civil-law terms are "immovables," "movables," and "corporeals," respectively. See N. Stephan Kinsella, "A Civil Law to Common Law Dictionary," *Louisiana Law Review* 54 (1994): 1265–305 for further differences between civil-law and common-law terminology. The term "things" is a broad civil-law concept that refers to all types of items, whether corporeal or incorporeal, movable or immovable.

²Debate over this issue manifests itself in differences over the issue of inalienability and with respect to the law of contract, i.e., can we "sell" or alienate our bodies in the same manner that we can alienate title to homesteaded property? For arguments against body inalienability, see N. Stephan Kinsella,

event, libertarians universally hold that all tangible scarce resources—whether homesteadable or created, immovable or movable, or our very bodies—are subject to rightful control, or "ownership," by specified individuals.

As we move away from the tangible (corporeal) toward the intangible, matters become fuzzier. Rights to reputations (defamation laws) and against blackmail, for example, are rights in very intangible types of things. Most, though not all, libertarians oppose laws against blackmail, and many oppose the idea of a right to one's reputation.[3]

Also disputed is the concept of intellectual property (herein referred to as IP). Are there individual rights to one's intellectual creations, such as inventions or written works? Should the legal system protect such rights? Below, I summarize current U.S. law on intellectual property rights. I then survey various libertarian views on IP rights, and present what I consider to be the proper view.

"A Theory of Contracts: Binding Promises, Title Transfer, and Inalienability" (paper presented at the Austrian Scholars Conference, Auburn, Alabama, April 1999); and N. Stephan Kinsella, "Inalienability and Punishment: A Reply to George Smith," *Journal of Libertarian Studies* 14, no. 1 (Winter 1998–99): 79–93. For arguments favoring such alienability, see Walter Block, "Toward a Libertarian Theory of Inalienability: A Critique of Rothbard, Barnett, Gordon, Smith, Kinsella, and Epstein," *Journal of Libertarian Studies* 17, no. 2 (Spring 2003): 39–85.

[3]For views in opposition to blackmail laws, see Walter Block, "Toward a Libertarian Theory of Blackmail," *Journal of Libertarian Studies* 15, no. 2 (Spring 2001); Walter Block, "A Libertarian Theory of Blackmail," *Irish Jurist* 33 (1998): 280–310; Walter Block, *Defending the Undefendable* (New York: Fleet Press, 1976), pp. 53–54; Murray N. Rothbard, *The Ethics of Liberty* (New York: New York University Press, 1998), pp. 124–26; and Eric Mack, "In Defense of Blackmail," *Philosophical Studies* 41 (1982): 274.

For libertarian views in favor of blackmail laws, see Robert Nozick, *Anarchy, State, and Utopia* (New York: Basic Books, 1974), pp. 85–86; and Richard Epstein, "Blackmail, Inc.," *University of Chicago Law Review* 50 (1983): 553.

For libertarian arguments against defamation (libel and slander) laws, see Block, *Defending the Undefendable*, pp. 50–53; and Rothbard, The Ethics of Liberty, pp. 126–28; in favor, see David Kelley in *David Kelley vs. Nat Hentoff: Libel Laws: Pro and Con*, audiotape (Free Press Association, Liberty Audio, 1987).

SUMMARY OF IP LAW

Types of IP

Intellectual property is a broad concept that covers several types of legally recognized rights arising from some type of intellectual creativity, or that are otherwise related to ideas.[4] IP rights are rights to intangible things[5]—to *ideas*, as expressed (copyrights), or as embodied in a practical implementation (patents). Tom Palmer puts it this way: "Intellectual property rights are rights in ideal objects, which are distinguished from the material substrata in which they are instantiated."[6] In today's legal systems, IP typically includes at least copyrights, trademarks, patents, and trade secrets.[7]

---

[4] In some European countries, the term "industrial property" is used instead of "intellectual property."

[5] *De La Vergne Refrigerating Mach. Co. v Featherstone*, 147 U.S. 209, 222, 13 S.Ct. 283, 285 (1893).

[6] Tom G. Palmer, "Are Patents and Copyrights Morally Justified? The Philosophy of Property Rights and Ideal Objects," in "Symposium: Intellectual Property," *Harvard Journal of Law & Public Policy* 13, no. 3 (Summer 1990): 818. As one commentator has noted, "intellectual property may be defined as embracing rights to novel ideas as contained in tangible products of cognitive effort." Dale A. Nance, "Foreword: Owning Ideas," in "Symposium: Intellectual Property," *Harvard Journal of Law & Public Policy* 13, no. 3 (Summer 1990): 757.

[7] A useful introduction to IP can be found in Arthur R. Miller and Michael H. Davis, *Intellectual Property: Patents, Trademarks, and Copyrights in a Nutshell*, 2nd ed. (St. Paul, Minn.: West Publishing, 1990); see also "Patent, Trademark, and Trade Secret," http://profs.lp.findlaw.com/patents/ index.html. For a good introduction to patent law, see Ronald B. Hildreth, *Patent Law: A Practitioner's Guide*, 3rd ed. (New York: Practising Law Institute, 1998). More in-depth treatises with further information on IP law include Donald S. Chisum, *Chisum on Patents* (New York: Matthew Bender, 2000); Melville B. Nimmer and David Nimmer, *Nimmer on Copyright* (New York: Matthew Bender, 2000); Paul Goldstein, *Copyright: Principles, Law, and Practice* (Boston: Little, Brown, 1989); J. Thomas McCarthy, *McCarthy on Trademarks and Unfair Competition*, 4th ed. (St. Paul, Minn.: West Group, 1996); and Roger M. Milgrim, *Milgrim on Trade Secrets* (New York:

Copyright

Copyright is a right given to authors of "original works," such as books, articles, movies, and computer programs. Copyright gives the exclusive right to reproduce the work, prepare derivative works, or to perform or present the work publicly.[8] Copyrights protect only the *form* or *expression* of ideas, not the underlying ideas themselves.[9]

While a copyright may be registered to obtain legal advantages, a copyright need not be registered to exist. Rather, a copyright comes into existence automatically the moment the work is "fixed" in a "tangible medium of expression," and lasts for the life of the author plus seventy years, or for a total of ninety-five years in cases in which the employer owns the copyright.[10]

Patent

A patent is a property right in inventions, that is, in devices or processes that perform a "useful" function.[11] A new or improved mousetrap is an example of a type of device which may be patented. A patent effectively grants the inventor a limited monopoly on the manufacture, use,

---

Matthew Bender, 2000). Useful information, brochures, and pamphlets are available from the United States Copyright Office, http://lcweb.loc.gov/copyright, and from the Patent and Trademark Office of the Department of Commerce, http://www.uspto.gov. Other useful sites are listed in this article's appendix and bibliography.

[8] 17 USC §§ 101, 106 *et pass.*

[9] Modern copyright law has superseded and largely preempted "common law copyright," which attached automatically from the moment of a work's creation, and which essentially conferred only a right of *first* publication. Goldstein, *Copyright*, §§ 15.4 *et seq.*

[10] 17 USC § 302. Due to recent legislation, these terms are twenty years longer than under previous law. See HR 2589, the *Sonny Bono Copyright Term Extension Act/Fairness in Music Licensing Act of 1998*.

[11] 35 USC § 1 *et seq.*; 37 CFR Part 1.

or sale of the invention. However, a patent actually only grants to the patentee the right to *exclude* (i.e., to prevent others from practicing the patented invention); it does not actually grant to the patentee the right to *use* the patented invention.[12]

Not every innovation or discovery is patentable. The U.S. Supreme Court has, for example, identified three categories of subject matter that are unpatentable, namely "laws of nature, natural phenomena, and abstract ideas."[13] Reducing abstract ideas to some type of "practical application," i.e., "a useful, concrete and tangible result,"[14] is patentable, however. U.S. patents, since June 8, 1995, last from the date of issuance until twenty years from the original filing date of the patent application[15] (the previous term was seventeen years from date of issue).

Trade Secret

A trade secret consists of any confidential formula, device, or piece of information which gives its holder a competitive advantage so long as it remains secret.[16] An

---

[12]Suppose *A* invents and patents a better mousetrap, which has a Nitinol (memory metal) spring for better snapping ability. Now suppose *B* invents and patents a mousetrap with a Nitinol spring covered with non-stick coating, to improve the ability to remove mouse remains while still providing the Nitinol-driven snapping action. *B* has to have a mousetrap with a Nitinol spring in order to use his invention, but this would infringe upon *A*'s patent. Similarly, *A* cannot add the non-stick coating to his own invention without infringing upon *B*'s improvement patent. In such situations, the two patentees may cross-license, so that *A* can practice *B*'s improvement to the mousetrap, and so *B* can use his own invention.

[13]*Diamond v Diehr*, 450 US 175, 185 (1981); see also 35 USC § 101.

[14]*In re Alappat*, 33 F3d 1526, 1544, 31 USPQ2d 1545, 1557 (Fed Cir 1994) (in banc). See also *State Street Bank & Trust Co. v Signature Financial Group*, 149 F3d 1368 (Fed Cir 1998).

[15]35 USC § 154(a)(2).

[16]See, e.g., R. Mark Halligan, esq., "Restatement of the Third Law—Unfair Competition: A Brief Summary," §§ 39–45, http://execpc.com/~

example would be the formula for Coca-Cola®. Trade secrets can include information that is not novel enough to be subject to patent protection, or not original enough to be protected by copyright (e.g., a database of seismic data or customer lists). Trade secret laws are used to prevent "misappropriations" of the trade secret, or to award damages for such misappropriations.[17] Trade secrets are protected under state law, although recent federal law has been enacted to prevent theft of trade secrets.[18]

Trade secret protection is obtained by declaring that the details of a subject are secret. The trade secret theoretically may last indefinitely, although disclosure, reverse-engineering, or independent invention may destroy it. Trade secrets can protect secret information and processes, e.g., compilations of data and maps not protectable by copyright, and can also be used to protect software source code not disclosed and not otherwise protectable by patent. One disadvantage of relying on trade secret protection is that a competitor who independently invents the subject of another's trade secret can obtain a patent on the device or process and actually prevent the original inventor (the trade secret holder) from using the invention.

Trademark

A trademark is a word, phrase, symbol, or design used to *identify* the source of goods or services sold, and to distinguish them from the goods or services of others. For example, the Coca-Cola® mark and the design that appears on their soft drink cans identifies them as products of that company, distinguishing them from competitors such as Pepsi®. Trademark law primarily prevents competitors

---

mhallign/unfair.html; also see the *Uniform Trade Secrets Act* (UTSA), http://nsi.org/Library/Espionage/usta.htm.

[17] See the *Uniform Trade Secrets Act* (UTSA).

[18] *Economic Espionage Act of 1996*, 18 USC §§ 1831–39.

from "infringing" upon the trademark, i.e., using "confusingly similar" marks to identify their own goods and services. Unlike copyrights and patents, trademark rights can last indefinitely if the owner continues to use the mark. The term of a federal trademark registration lasts ten years, with ten-year renewal terms being available.[19]

Other rights related to trademark protection include rights against trademark dilution,[20] certain forms of cybersquatting,[21] and various "unfair competition" claims. IP also includes recent legal innovations, such as the mask work protection available for semiconductor integrated circuit (IC) designs,[22] the *sui generis* protection, similar to copyright, for boat hull designs,[23] and the proposed *sui generis* right in databases, or collections of information.[24]

In the United States, federal law almost exclusively governs copyrights and patents, since the Constitution grants Congress the power "to promote the progress of science and useful arts."[25] Despite the federal source of patents and copyrights, various related aspects, such as *ownership* of patents, are based on state law, which nevertheless tend to be fairly uniform from state to state.[26] Federal trademarks,

---

[19] 15 USC § 1501 *et seq.*; 37 CFR Part 2.

[20] 15 USC §§ 1125(c), 1127.

[21] 15 USC § 1125(d); *Anticybersquatting Consumer Protection Act*, PL 106–113 (1999); HR 3194, S1948.

[22] See 17 USC § 901 *et seq.*

[23] See 17 USC § 1301 *et seq.*

[24] See, e.g., HR 354 (introduced 1/19/1999), *Collections of Information Antipiracy Act*. See also Jane C. Ginsburg, "Copyright, Common Law, and *Sui Generis* Protection of Databases in the United States and Abroad," *University of Cincinnati Law Review* 66 (1997): 151.

[25] U.S. Cons., Art I, § 8; *Kewanee Oil Co. v. Bicron Corp.*, 415 US 470, 479, 94 S.Ct. 1879, 1885 (1974).

[26] See Paul C. van Slyke and Mark M. Friedman, "Employer's Rights to Inventions and Patents of Its Officers, Directors, and Employees," *AIPLA Quarterly Journal* 18 (1990): 127; and *Chisum on Patents*, § 22.03; 17 USC §§ 101, 201.

by contrast, not being explicitly authorized in the Constitution, are based on the interstate commerce clause and thus only covers marks for goods and services in interstate commerce.[27] State trademarks still exist since they have not been completely preempted by federal law, but federal marks tend to be more commercially important and powerful. Trade secrets are generally protected under state, not federal, law.[28]

Many laymen, including libertarians, have a poor understanding of IP concepts and law, and often confuse copyrights, trademarks, and patents. It is widely, and incorrectly, believed that in the U.S. system, the inventor who files first at the patent office has priority over those who file later. However, the U.S. system is actually a "first-to-invent" system, unlike most other countries, which do have a "first-to-file" system for priority.[29]

IP Rights and Relation to Tangible Property

As noted above, IP rights, at least for patents and copyrights, may be considered rights in ideal objects. It is

---

[27]U.S. Constitution, art. 1, sec. 8, clause 3; *Wickard v Filburn*, 317 US 111, 63 S. Ct. 82 (1942).

[28]But see the federal *Economic Espionage Act of 1996*, 18 USC §§ 1831–39.

[29]Ayn Rand mistakenly assumes that the first to file has priority (and then she is at pains to defend such a system). See Ayn Rand, "Patents and Copyrights," in *Capitalism: The Unknown Ideal* (New York: New American Library, 1967), p. 133. She also confusingly attacks the strict antitrust scrutiny given to patent holders. However, since patents are government-grant-ed monopolies, it is not unjust to use an anti-monopoly law to limit the ability of a patent owner to extend this monopoly beyond the bounds intended by the patent statute. The problem with antitrust laws is in their application to normal, peaceful business dealings, not to limit real—i.e., government-granted—monopolies. A similar point might be made with regard to Bill Gates, whose fortune has largely been built based on the government-granted monopoly inherent in copyright. Moreover, as Bill Gates is no libertarian, and doubtlessly does not oppose the legitimacy of antitrust laws, one can hardly wring one's hands in pity over his having to lie in the very bed he helped make.

important to point out that ownership of an idea, or ideal object, effectively gives the IP owners a property right in *every* physical embodiment of that work or invention. Consider a copyrighted book. Copyright holder A has a right to the underlying ideal object, of which the book is but one example. The copyright system gives A the right in the very *pattern* of words in the book; therefore, by implication, A has a right to *every* tangible instantiation or embodiment of the book—i.e., a right in every physical version of the book, or, at least, to every book within the jurisdiction of the legal system that recognizes the copyright.

Thus, if A writes a novel, he has a copyright in this "work." If he sells a physical copy of the novel to B, in book form, then B owns only that one physical copy of the novel; B does not own the "novel" itself, and is not entitled to make a copy of the novel, even using his own paper and ink. Thus, even if B owns the material property of paper and printing press, he cannot use his own property to create another copy of A's book. Only A has the *right* to *copy* the book (hence, "copyright").

Likewise, A's ownership of a patent gives him the right to prevent a third party from using or practicing the patented invention, even if the third party only uses his own property. In this way, A's ownership of ideal rights gives him some degree of control—ownership—over the tangible property of innumerable others. Patent and copyright invariably transfer partial ownership of tangible property from its natural owner to innovators, inventors, and artists.

LIBERTARIAN PERSPECTIVES ON IP

The Spectrum

Libertarian views on IP range from complete support of the fullest gamut of IP imaginable, to outright opposition to IP rights. Most of the debate about IP concerns patent and copyright; as discussed below, trademark and trade secret are less problematic. Therefore, this article focuses primarily on the legitimacy of patent and copyright.

Pro-IP arguments may be divided into natural-rights and utilitarian arguments. Libertarian IP advocates tend to adopt the former justification.[30] For example, natural-rights, or at least not explicitly utilitarian, libertarian proponents of IP include, from more to less extreme, Galambos, Schulman, and Rand.[31] Among precursors to modern

---

[30] For conventional theories of intellectual property, see "Bibliography of General Theories of Intellectual Property," *Encyclopedia of Law and Economics*, http://encyclo.findlaw.com/biblio/1600.htm; and Edmund Kitch, "The Nature and Function of the Patent System," *Journal of Law and Economics* 20 (1977): 265.

[31] See Andrew J. Galambos, *The Theory of Volition*, vol. 1, ed. Peter N. Sisco (San Diego: Universal Scientific Publications, 1999); J. Neil Schulman, "Informational Property: Logorights," *Journal of Social and Biological Structures* (1990); and Rand, "Patents and Copyrights." Other Objectivists (Randians) who support IP include George Reisman, *Capitalism: A Treatise on Economics* (Ottawa, Ill.: Jameson Books, 1996), pp. 388–89; David Kelley, "Response to Kinsella," *IOS Journal* 5, no. 2 (June 1995): 13, in response to N. Stephan Kinsella, "Letter on Intellectual Property Rights," *IOS Journal* 5, no. 2 (June 1995): 12–13; Murray I. Franck, "Ayn Rand, Intellectual Property Rights, and Human Liberty," 2 audio tapes, Institute for Objectivist Studies Lecture; Laissez-Faire Books (1991); Murray I. Franck, "Intellectual Property Rights: Are Intangibles True Property," *IOS Journal* 5, no. 1 (April 1995); and Murray I. Franck, "Intellectual and Personality Property," *IOS Journal* 5, no. 3 (September 1995): 7, in response to Kinsella, "Letter on Intellectual Property Rights." It is difficult to find published discussions of Galambos's idea, apparently because his own theories bizarrely restrict the ability of his supporters to disseminate them. See, e.g., Jerome Tuccille, *It Usually Begins with Ayn Rand* (San Francisco: Cobden Press, 1971), pp. 69–71. Scattered references to and discussions of Galambos's theories may be found, however, in David Friedman, "In Defense of Private Orderings: Comments on

libertarians, Spooner and Spencer both advocated IP on moral or natural-rights grounds.[32]

According to the natural-rights view of IP held by some libertarians, creations of the mind are entitled to protection just as tangible property is. Both are the product of one's labor and one's mind. Because one owns one's labor, one has a

> natural law right to the fruit of one's labor. Under this view, just as one has a right to the crops one plants, so one has a right to the ideas one generates and the art one produces.[33]

This theory depends on the notion that one owns one's body and labor, and therefore, its fruits, including intellectual "creations." An individual creates a sonnet, a song, a sculpture, by employing his own labor and body. He is thus entitled to "own" these creations, because they result from other things he "owns."

There are also utilitarian pro-IP arguments. Federal Judge Richard Posner is one prominent utilitarian (although not libertarian) IP advocate.[34] Among libertarians, anarchist David Friedman analyzes and appears to

---

Julie Cohen's 'Copyright and the Jurisprudence of Self-Help'," *Berkeley Technology Law Journal* 13, no. 3 (Fall 1998): n. 52; and in Stephen Foerster, "The Basics of Economic Government," http://www.economic.net/articles/ar0001.html.

[32] Lysander Spooner, "The Law of Intellectual Property: or An Essay on the Right of Authors and Inventors to a Perpetual Property in Their Ideas," in *The Collected Works of Lysander Spooner*, vol. 3, ed. Charles Shively (1855; reprint, Weston, Mass.: M&S Press, 1971); Herbert Spencer, *The Principles of Ethics*, vol. 2 (1893; reprint, Indianapolis, Ind.: Liberty Press, 1978), part IV, chap. 13, p. 121. See also Wendy McElroy, "Intellectual Property: Copyright and Patent," http://www.zetetics.com/mac/intpro1.htm and http://www.zetetics.com/mac/intpro2.htm; and Palmer, "Are Patents and Copyrights Morally Justified?" pp. 818, 825.

[33] Palmer, "Are Patents and Copyrights Morally Justified?" p. 819.

[34] Richard A. Posner, *Economic Analysis of Law*, 4th ed. (Boston: Little, Brown, 1992), § 3.3, pp. 38–45.

endorse IP on "law-and-economics" grounds,[35] a utilitarian institutional framework. The utilitarian argument presupposes that we should choose laws and policies that maximize "wealth" or "utility." With respect to copyright and patent, the idea is that more artistic and inventive "innovation" corresponds with, or leads to, more wealth. Public goods and free-rider effects reduce the amount of such wealth below its optimal level, i.e., lower than the level we would achieve if there were adequate IP laws on the books. Thus, wealth is optimized, or at least increased, by granting copyright and patent monopolies that encourage authors and inventors to innovate and create.[36]

On the other hand, there is a long tradition of opposition to patent and copyright. Modern opponents include Rothbard, McElroy, Palmer, Lepage, Bouckaert, and myself.[37] Benjamin Tucker also vigorously opposed IP in a

---

[35] David D. Friedman, "Standards As Intellectual Property: An Economic Approach," *University of Dayton Law Review* 19, no. 3 (Spring 1994): 1109–29; and David D. Friedman, *Law's Order: What Economics Has to Do with Law and Why it Matters* (Princeton, N.J.: Princeton University Press, 2000), chap. 11. Ejan Mackaay also advocates IP on utilitarian grounds, in "Economic Incentives in Markets for Information and Innovation," in "Symposium: Intellectual Property," *Harvard Journal of Law & Public Policy* 13, no. 3, p. 867. Earlier utilitarian advocates of IP include John Stuart Mill and Jeremy Bentham. See Arnold Plant, "The Economic Theory Concerning Patents for Inventions," in *Selected Economic Essays and Addresses* (London: Routledge & Kegan Paul, 1974), p. 44; Roger E. Meiners and Robert J. Staaf, "Patents, Copyrights, and Trademarks: Property or Monopoly?" in "Symposium: Intellectual Property," *Harvard Journal of Law & Public Policy* 13, no. 3, p. 911.

[36] See Palmer, "Are Patents and Copyrights Morally Justified?" pp. 820–21; Julio H. Cole, "Patents and Copyrights: Do the Benefits Exceed the Costs?" http://www.economia.ufm.edu.gt/Catedraticos/jhcole/Cole%20_MPS_.pdf

[37] See Murray N. Rothbard, *Man, Economy, and State* (Los Angeles: Nash Publishing, 1962), pp. 652–60; Murray N. Rothbard, *The Ethics of Liberty*, pp. 123–24; Wendy McElroy, "Contra Copyright," *The Voluntaryist* (June 1985); McElroy, "Intellectual Property: Copyright and Patent"; Tom G. Palmer, "Intellectual Property: A Non-Posnerian Law and Economics Approach," *Hamline Law Review* 12 (1989): 261; Palmer, "Are Patents and Copyrights Morally Justified?"; on Lepage, see Mackaay, "Economic Incentives," p. 869; Boudewijn

debate in the nineteenth century individualist-anarchist periodical *Liberty*.³⁸ These commentators point out the many problems with conventional utilitarian and natural-rights arguments given to justify IP rights. These and other shortcomings of standard pro-IP arguments are surveyed below.

Utilitarian Defenses of IP

Advocates of IP often justify it on utilitarian grounds. Utilitarians hold that the "end" of encouraging more innovation and creativity justifies the seemingly immoral

---

Bouckaert, "What is Property?" in "Symposium: Intellectual Property," *Harvard Journal of Law & Public Policy* 13, no. 3, p. 775; N. Stephan Kinsella, "Is Intellectual Property Legitimate?" *Pennsylvania Bar Association Intellectual Property Law Newsletter* 1, no. 2 (Winter 1998): 3; Kinsella, "Letter on Intellectual Property Rights," and "In Defense of Napster and Against the Second Homesteading Rule."

F.A. Hayek also appears to be opposed to patents. See *The Collected Works of F.A. Hayek*, vol. 1, *The Fatal Conceit: The Errors of Socialism*, ed. W.W. Bartley (Chicago: University of Chicago Press, 1989), p. 6; and Meiners and Staaf, "Patents, Copyrights, and Trademarks," p. 911. Cole challenges the utilitarian justification for patents and copyright in "Patents and Copyrights: Do the Benefits Exceed the Costs?" See also Fritz Machlup, U.S. Senate Subcommittee On Patents, Trademarks & Copyrights, *An Economic Review of the Patent System*, 85th Cong., 2nd Session, 1958, Study No. 15; Fritz Machlup and Edith Penrose, "The Patent Controversy in the Nineteenth Century," *Journal of Economic History* 10 (1950): 1; Roderick T. Long, "The Libertarian Case Against Intellectual Property Rights," *Formulations* 3, no. 1 (Autumn 1995); Stephen Breyer, "The Uneasy Case for Copyright: A Study of Copyright in Books, Photocopies, and Computer Programs," *Harvard Law Review* 84 (1970): 281; Wendy J. Gordon, "An Inquiry into the Merits of Copyright: The Challenges of Consistency, Consent, and Encouragement Theory," *Stanford Law Review* 41 (1989): 1343; and Jesse Walker, "Copy Catfight: How Intellectual Property Laws Stifle Popular Culture," *Reason* (March 2000).

³⁸McElroy, "Intellectual Property: Copyright and Patent." Also strongly opposed to IP was the nineteenth-century Jacksonian editorialist William Leggett. See Palmer, "Are Patents and Copyrights Morally Justified?" pp. 818, 828–29. Ludwig von Mises expressed no opinion on the issue, merely drawing the economic implications from the presence or absence of such laws. See *Human Action*, 3rd rev. ed. (Chicago: Henry Regnery, 1966), chap. 23, section 6, pp. 661–62.

"means" of restricting the freedom of individuals to use their physical property as they see fit. But there are three fundamental problems with justifying any right or law on strictly utilitarian grounds.

First, let us suppose that wealth or utility could be maximized by adopting certain legal rules; the "size of the pie" is increased. Even then, this does not show that these rules are justified. For example, one could argue that net utility is enhanced by redistributing half of the wealth of society's richest one percent to its poorest ten percent. But even if stealing some of A's property and giving it to B increases B's welfare "more" than it diminishes A's (if such a comparison could, somehow, be made), this does not establish that the theft of A's property is justified. Wealth maximization is not the goal of law; rather, the goal is justice—giving each man his due.[39] Even if overall wealth is increased due to IP laws, it does not follow that this allegedly desirable result justifies the unethical violation of some individuals' rights to use their own property as they see fit.

In addition to ethical problems, utilitarianism is not coherent. It necessarily involves making illegitimate interpersonal utility comparisons, as when the "costs" of IP laws are subtracted from the "benefits" to determine whether such laws are a net benefit.[40] But not all values

---

[39] According to Justinian, "Justice is the constant and perpetual wis h to render every one his due. . . . The maxims of law are these: to live honestly, to hurt no one, to give every one his due." *The Institutes of Justinian: Text, Translation, and Commentary*, trans. J.A.C. Thomas (Amsterdam: North-Holland, 1975).

[40] On the defects of utilitarianism and interpersonal utility comparisons, see Murray N. Rothbard, "Praxeology, Value Judgments, and Public Policy," in *The Logic of Action One* (Cheltenham, U.K.: Edward Elgar, 1997), esp. pp. 90–99; Rothbard, "Toward a Reconstruction of Utility and Welfare Economics," in The Logic of Action One; Anthony de Jasay, *Against Politics: On Government, Anarchy, and Order* (London: Routledge, 1997), pp. 81–82, 92, 98, 144, 149–51.

On scientism and empiricism, see Rothbard, "The Mantle of Science," in *The Logic of Action One*; Hans-Hermann Hoppe, "In Defense of Extreme Rationalism:

have a market price; in fact, none of them do. Mises showed that even for goods that have a market price, the price does not serve as a *measure* of the good's value.[41]

Finally, even if we set aside the problems of interpersonal utility comparisons and the justice of redistribution and we plow ahead, employing standard utilitarian measurement techniques, it is not at all clear that IP laws lead to any change—either an increase or a decrease—in overall wealth.[42] It is debatable whether copyrights and patents really are necessary to encourage the production of creative works and inventions, or that the incremental gains in innovation outweigh the immense costs of an IP system. Econometric studies do not conclusively show net gains in

---

Thoughts on Donald McCloskey's *The Rhetoric of Economics*," *Review of Austrian Economics* 3 (1989): 179.

On epistemological dualism, see Ludwig von Mises, *The Ultimate Foundation of Economic Science: An Essay on Method*, 2nd ed. (Kansas City: Sheed Andrews and McMeel, 1962); Ludwig von Mises, *Epistemological Problems of Economics*, trans. George Reisman (New York: New York University Press, 1981); Hans-Hermann Hoppe, *Economic Science and the Austrian Method* (Auburn, Ala.: Ludwig von Mises Institute, 1995); and Hoppe, "In Defense of Extreme Rationalism."

[41]Mises states: "Although it is usual to speak of money as a measure of value and prices, the notion is entirely fallacious. So long as the subjective theory of value is accepted, this question of measurement cannot arise." "On the Measurement of Value," in *The Theory of Money and Credit*, trans. H.E. Batson (1912; reprint, Indianapolis, Ind.: Liberty Fund, 1980), p. 51. Also: "Money is neither a yardstick of value nor of prices. Money does not measure value. Nor are prices measured in money: they are amounts of money." Ludwig von Mises, *Socialism: An Economic and Sociological Analysis*, 3rd rev. ed., trans. J. Kahane (Indianapolis, Ind.: Liberty Press, 1981), p. 99; see also Mises, *Human Action*, pp. 96, 122, 204, 210, 217, and 289.

[42]For an excellent survey and critique of the cost-benefit justification for patent and copyright, see Cole, "Patents and Copyrights: Do the Benefits Exceed the Costs?" For useful discussions of evidence in this regard, see Palmer, "Intellectual Property: A Non-Posnerian Law and Economics Approach," pp. 300–2; Palmer, "Are Patents and Copyrights Morally Justified?" pp. 820–21, 850–51; Bouckaert, "What is Property?" pp. 812–13; Leonard Prusak, "Does the Patent System Have Measurable Economic Value?" *AIPLA Quarterly Journal* 10 (1982): 50–59; and Leonard Prusak, "The Economic Theory Concerning Patents and Inventions," *Economica 1* (1934): 30–51.

wealth. Perhaps there would even be *more* innovation if there were no patent laws; maybe more money for research and development (R&D) would be available if it were not being spent on patents and lawsuits. It is possible that companies would have an even greater incentive to innovate if they could not rely on a near twenty-year monopoly.[43]

There are undoubtedly costs of the patent system. As noted, patents can be obtained only for "practical" applications of ideas, but not for more abstract or theoretical ideas. This skews resources away from theoretical R&D.[44] It is not clear that society is better off with relatively more practical invention and relatively less theoretical research and development. Additionally, many inventions are patented for defensive reasons, resulting in patent lawyers' salaries and patent office fees. This large overhead would be unnecessary if there were no patents. In the absence of patent laws, for example, companies would not spend money obtaining or defending against such ridiculous patents as those in the Appendix. It simply has not been shown that IP leads to net gains in wealth. But should not those who advocate the use of force against others' property have to satisfy a burden of proof?

---

[43] See Cole, "Patents and Copyrights: Do the Benefits Exceed the Costs?" for further examples of costs of patent and copyright laws.

[44] Plant, "The Economic Theory Concerning Patents for Inventions," p. 43. See also Rothbard, *Man, Economy, and State*, pp. 658–59:

> It is by no means self-evident that patents encourage an increased absolute quantity of research expenditures. But certainly patents distort the *type* of research expenditure being conducted.... Research expenditures are therefore *overstimulated* in the early stages before anyone has a patent, and they are *unduly restricted* in the period after the patent is received. In addition, some inventions are considered patentable, while others are not. The patent system then has the further effect of artificially stimulating research expenditures in the *patentable* areas, while artificially restricting research in the *nonpatentable* areas.

We must remember that when we advocate certain rights and laws, and inquire into their legitimacy, we are inquiring into the legitimacy and ethics of the use of *force*. To ask whether a law should be enacted or exist is to ask: is it proper to use force against certain people in certain circumstances? It is no wonder that this question is not really addressed by analysis of wealth maximization. Utilitarian analysis is thoroughly confused and bankrupt: talk about increasing the size of the pie is methodologically flawed; there is no clear evidence that the pie increases with IP rights. Further, pie growth does not justify the use of force against the otherwise legitimate property of others. For these reasons, utilitarian IP defenses are unpersuasive.

Some Problems with Natural Rights

Other libertarian proponents of IP argue that certain ideas deserve protection as property rights because they are *created*. Rand supported patents and copyrights as "the legal implementation of the base of all property rights: a man's right to the product of his mind."[45] For Rand, IP rights are, in a sense, the reward for productive work. It is only fair that a creator reap the benefits of others using his creation. For this reason, in part, she opposes *perpetual* patent and copyright—because future, unborn heirs of the original creator are not themselves responsible for the creation of their ancestors' work.

One problem with the creation-based approach is that it almost invariably protects only *certain types* of creations—unless, that is, every single useful idea one comes up with is subject to ownership (more on this below). But the distinction between the protectable and the unprotectable is necessarily arbitrary. For example, philosophical or mathematical or scientific truths cannot be protected under

---

[45] Rand, "Patents and Copyrights," p. 130.

current law on the grounds that commerce and social intercourse would grind to a halt were every new phrase, philosophical truth, and the like considered the exclusive property of its creator. For this reason, patents can be obtained only for so-called "practical applications" of ideas, but not for more abstract or theoretical ideas. Rand agrees with this disparate treatment, in attempting to distinguish between an unpatentable *discovery* and a patentable *invention*. She argues that a "scientific or philosophical discovery, which identifies a law of nature, a principle or a fact of reality not previously known" is not *created* by the discoverer.

But the distinction between creation and discovery is not clearcut or rigorous.[46] Nor is it clear why such a distinction, even if clear, is ethically relevant in defining property rights. No one creates *matter*; they just manipulate and grapple with it according to physical laws. In this sense, no one really creates *anything*. They merely rearrange matter into new arrangements and patterns. An engineer who invents a new mousetrap has rearranged existing parts to provide a function not previously performed. Others who learn of this new arrangement can now also make an improved mousetrap. Yet the mousetrap merely follows laws of nature. The inventor did not invent the matter out of which the mousetrap is made, nor the *facts* and laws exploited to make it work.

---

[46]Plant is correct in stating that "[t]he task of distinguishing a scientific discovery from its practical application, which may be patentable . . . is often baffling to the most subtle lawyer." "The Economic Theory Concerning Patents for Inventions," pp. 49–50. On a related note, the U.S. Supreme Court has noted that "[t]he specification and claims of a patent . . . constitute one of the most difficult legal instruments to draw with accuracy." *Topliff v Topliff*, 145 US 156, 171, 12 S.Ct. 825 (1892). Perhaps this is because patent law has no moorings to objective borders of actual, tangible property, and thus is inherently vague, amorphous, ambiguous, and subjective. For the latter reason alone, one would think that Objectivists—ardent, self-proclaimed defenders of objectivity and opponents of subjectivism—would oppose patent and copyright.

Similarly, Einstein's "discovery" of the relation $E=mc^2$, once known by others, allows them to manipulate matter in a more efficient way. Without Einstein's, or the inventor's, efforts, others would have been *ignorant* of certain causal laws, of ways matter can be manipulated and utilized. Both the inventor and the theoretical scientist engage in creative mental effort to produce useful, new ideas. Yet one is rewarded, and the other is not. In one recent case, the inventor of a new way to calculate a number representing the shortest path between two points—an extremely useful technique—was not given patent protection because this was "merely" a mathematical algorithm.[47] But it is arbitrary and unfair to reward more practical inventors and entertainment providers, such as the engineer and songwriter, and to leave more theoretical science and math researchers and philosophers unrewarded. The distinction is inherently vague, arbitrary, and unjust.

Moreover, adopting a limited term for IP rights, as opposed to a perpetual right, also requires arbitrary rules. For example, patents last for twenty years from the filing date, while copyrights last, in the case of individual authors, for seventy years past the author's death. No one can seriously maintain that nineteen years for a patent is too short, and twenty-one years too long, any more than the current price for a gallon of milk can be objectively classified as too low or too high.

Thus, one problem with the natural-rights approach to validating IP is that it necessarily involves arbitrary distinctions

---

[47] *In re Trovato*, 33 USPQ2d 1194 (Fed Cir 1994). Recent case law has expanded the types of mathematical and computer algorithms and business methods that can be protected by patent. See, e.g., *State Street Bank & Trust Co. v Signature Financial Group*, 149 F3d 1368 (Fed Cir 1998). However, no matter where the line is drawn between unpatentable "laws of nature" and "abstract ideas" and patentable "practical applications," patent law still necessarily makes a distinction between the two.

with respect to what classes of creations deserve protection, and concerning the length of the term of the protection.

Of course, one way to avoid this difficulty is to claim that *everything* is protectable by IP, with perpetual (infinite) terms. Spooner,[48] for example, advocated perpetual rights for patent and copyright. Schulman advocates a much broader concept of creations or ideas protectable by IP. He argues for property rights called "logorights" in any "logos" that one creates. The logos is the "material identity" or identity-pattern of created things. The owner of a logos would own the order or pattern of information imposed upon, or observed in, material substances.

The most radical of all IP proponents is Andrew Joseph Galambos, whose ideas, to the extent that I understand them, border on the absurd.[49] Galambos believed that man has property rights in his own life (primordial property) and in all "non-procreative derivatives of his life."[50] Since the "first derivatives" of a man's life are his thoughts and ideas, thoughts and ideas are "primary property." Since action is based on primary property (ideas), actions are owned as well; this is referred to as "liberty." Secondary derivatives, such as land, televisions, and other tangible goods, are produced by ideas and action. Thus, property

---

[48] Spooner, "The Law of Intellectual Property"; McElroy, "Intellectual Property: Copyright and Patent"; Palmer, "Are Patents and Copyrights Morally Justified?" pp. 818, 825.

[49] See Galambos, *The Theory of Volition*, vol. 1. Evan R. Soulé, Jr., "What Is Volitional Science?" http://www.tuspco.com/html/what_is_v-50_.html. I have read only sketchy accounts of Galambos's theories. I also met a real, live Galambosian once, much to my surprise (I had supposed that they were fictional creations of Tuccille [*It Usually Begins with Ayn Rand*, pp. 69–71]), at a Mises Institute conference a few years ago. My criticism of Galambos's ideas in what follows only applies to the extent that I am properly describing his views.

[50] Friedman, "In Defense of Private Orderings," n. 52; Foerster, "The Basics of Economic Government."

rights in tangible items are relegated to lowly secondary status, as compared with the "primary" status of property rights in ideas. (Even Rand once elevated patents over mere property rights in tangible goods, in her bizarre notion that "patents are the heart and core of property rights."[51] Can we really believe that there were no property rights respected before the 1800s, when patent rights became systematized?)

Galambos reportedly took his own ideas to ridiculous lengths, claiming a property right in his own ideas and requiring his students not to repeat them;[52] dropping a nickel in a fund box every time he used the word "liberty," as a royalty to the descendants of Thomas Paine, the alleged "inventor" of the word "liberty"; and changing his original name from Joseph Andrew Galambos (Jr., presumably) to Andrew Joseph Galambos, to avoid infringing his identically-named father's rights to the name.[53]

By widening the scope of IP, and by lengthening its duration to avoid making such arbitrary distinctions as Rand does, the absurdity and injustice caused by IP becomes even more pronounced (as Galambos demonstrates). And by extending the term of patents and copyrights to infinity, subsequent generations would be choked by ever-growing restraints on their own use of property. No one would be able to manufacture—or even use—a light bulb without getting permission from Edison's heirs. No one would even be able to build a house without getting permission from the heirs of the first protohuman who left the caves and built a hut. No one could use a variety

---

[51]Rand, "Patents and Copyrights," p. 133.

[52]Friedman, "In Defense of Private Orderings," n. 52.

[53]Tuccille, *It Usually Begins with Ayn Rand*, p. 70. Of course, I suppose that any Galambosian other than Galambos himself, having the same type of dilemma, would be unable to change his name as a solution to the problem, because this solution was Galambos's inalienable, "absolute" idea.

of life-saving techniques, chemicals, or treatments without obtaining permission of various lucky, rich descendants. No one would be able to boil water to purify it, or use pickling to preserve foods, unless he is granted license by the originators (or their distant heirs) of such techniques.

Such unbounded ideal rights would pose a serious threat to tangible-property rights, and would threaten to overwhelm them. All use of tangible property would by now be impossible, as every conceivable use of property, every single action, would be bound to infringe upon one of the millions of past, accreted IP rights, and the human race would die of starvation. But, as Rand noted, men are not ghosts; we have a spiritual aspect, but also a physical one.[54] Any system that elevates rights in ideas to such an extreme that it overrides rights in tangible things is clearly not a suitable ethical system for living, breathing human beings. No one living can actually act in accordance with such an unrestricted view of IP. The remaining advocates of IP all qualify their endorsement by limiting the scope and/or terms of IP rights, thus adopting the ethically arbitrary distinctions noted above.

A deeper problem for the natural-rights position lies in its undue emphasis on "creation," instead of scarcity, as giving rise to property rights, as discussed below.

IP AND PROPERTY RIGHTS

Property and Scarcity

Let us take a step back and look afresh at the idea of property rights. Libertarians believe in property rights in tangible goods (resources). Why? What is it about tangible

---

[54]Harry Binswanger, ed., *The Ayn Rand Lexicon: Objectivism from A to Z* (New York: New American Library, 1986), pp. 326–27, 467.

goods that makes them subjects for property rights? Why are tangible goods property?

A little reflection will show that it is these goods' *scarcity*—the fact that there can be *conflict* over these goods by multiple human actors. The very possibility of conflict over a resource renders it scarce, giving rise to the need for ethical rules to govern its use. Thus, the fundamental social and ethical function of property rights is to prevent interpersonal conflict over scarce resources.[55] As Hoppe notes:

> [O]nly because scarcity exists is there even a problem of formulating moral laws; insofar as goods are superabundant ("free" goods), no conflict over the use of goods is possible and no action-coordination is needed. Hence, it follows that any ethic, correctly conceived, must be formulated as a theory of property, i.e., a theory of the assignment of rights of exclusive control over scarce means. Because only then does it become possible to avoid otherwise inescapable and unresolvable conflict.[56]

Others who recognize the importance of scarcity in defining what property is include Plant, Hume, Palmer, Rothbard, and Tucker.[57]

---

[55] The fundamental economic, or catallactic, role for private property rights, along with money prices arising from exchanges of property, is to permit *economic calculation*. See N. Stephan Kinsella, "Knowledge, Calculation, Conflict, and Law: Review Essay of Randy E. Barnett, *The Structure of Liberty: Justice and the Rule of Law*," *Quarterly Journal of Austrian Economics* 2, no. 4 (Winter 1999): 49–71.

[56] Hans-Hermann Hoppe, *A Theory of Socialism and Capitalism* (Boston: Kluwer Academic Publishers, 1989), p. 235 n. 9.

[57] Plant, "The Economic Theory Concerning Patents for Inventions," pp. 35–36; David Hume, *An Inquiry Concerning the Principles of Morals: With a Supplement: A Dialogue* (1751; reprint, New York: Liberal Arts Press, 1957); Palmer, "Intellectual Property: A Non-Posnerian Law and Economics Approach," pp. 261–66 and n. 50 (distinguishing between "static" and "dynamic" scarcity), also pp. 279–80; Palmer, "Are Patents and Copyrights Morally Justified?" pp. 860–61, 864–65; and Rothbard, "Justice and Property Rights," in *The Logic of Action One*, p. 274; on Tucker, see McElroy, "Intellectual Property: Copyright and Patent."

Nature, then, contains things that are economically scarce. My use of such a thing *conflicts* with (excludes) your use of it, and vice versa. The function of property rights is to prevent interpersonal conflict over scarce resources, by allocating exclusive ownership of resources to specified individuals (owners). To perform this function, property rights must be both *visible* and *just*. Clearly, in order for individuals to avoid using property owned by others, property borders and property rights must be objective (intersubjectively ascertainable); they must be *visible*.[58] For this reason, property rights must be objective and unambiguous. In other words, "good fences make good neighbors."[59]

Property rights must be demonstrably *just*, as well as visible, because they cannot serve their function of preventing conflict unless they are acceptable as fair by those affected by the rules.[60] If property rights are allocated unfairly, or simply grabbed by force, this is like having no property rights at all; it is merely might versus right again, i.e., the pre-property rights situation. But as libertarians recognize, following Locke, it is only the first occupier or user of such property that can be its natural owner. Only the *first-occupier* homesteading rule provides an objective, ethical, and nonarbitrary allocation of ownership in scarce resources.[61]

---

[58]Hoppe, *A Theory of Socialism and Capitalism*, pp. 140–41. I do not mean to restrict rights to the sighted; the term "visible" here means observable or discernible. I owe this clarification to Gene Callahan.

[59]Robert Frost, "The Mending Wall," in North of Boston, 2nd ed. (New York: Henry Holt, 1915), pp. 11–13. (Please do not e-mail me about this. I do not care what Frost "really" meant in that poem. I just like the saying.)

[60]Hoppe, *A Theory of Socialism and Capitalism*, p. 138.

[61]See, on the proper approach to homesteading and the first-user rule (the prior-later distinction), Hoppe, *A Theory of Socialism and Capitalism*, pp. 141–44; Hoppe, *The Economics and Ethics of Private Property* (Boston: Kluwer Academic Publishers, 1993), pp. 191–93; Jeffrey M. Herbener, "The Pareto Rule and Welfare Economics," *Review of Austrian Economics* 10, no. 1 (1997): 105: "Once the item is owned by the first-user, others no longer have the option of being its

When property rights in scarce means are allocated in accordance with first-occupier homesteading rules, property borders are visible, and the allocation is demonstrably just. Conflict can be avoided with such property rights in place because third parties can see and, thus, sidestep the property borders, and be motivated to do so because the allocation is just and fair.

But surely it is clear, given the origin, justification, and function of property rights, that they are applicable only to *scarce* resources. Were we in a Garden of Eden where land and other goods were infinitely abundant, there would be no scarcity and, therefore, no need for property rules; property concepts would be meaningless. The idea of conflict, and the idea of rights, would not even arise. For example, your taking my lawnmower would not really deprive me of it if I could conjure up another in the blink of an eye. Lawnmower-taking in these circumstances would not be "theft." Property rights are not applicable to things of infinite abundance, because there cannot be conflict over such things.

Thus, property rights must have objective, discernible borders, and must be allocated in accordance with the first-occupier homesteading rule. Moreover, property rights can apply only to scarce resources. The problem with IP rights is that the ideal objects protected by IP rights are not scarce; and, further, that such property rights are not, and

---

first-user; thus, their preferences at that point in time have no bearing on the Pareto-superior nature of the acquisition by the first-user"; and de Jasay, *Against Politics*, pp. 172–79. On the ethical justifications of such a property-rights scheme, see Hoppe, *A Theory of Socialism and Capitalism*, chap. 7; Hoppe, *The Economics and Ethics of Private Property*; Rothbard, *The Ethics of Liberty*; Rothbard, "Justice and Property Rights," in *The Logic of Action One*; N. Stephan Kinsella, "A Libertarian Theory of Punishment and Rights" *Loyola of Los Angeles Law Review* 30 (Spring 1996): 607; N. Stephan Kinsella, "New Rationalist Directions in Libertarian Rights Theory," *Journal of Libertarian Studies* 12, no. 2 (Fall 1996): 313–26.

cannot be, allocated in accordance with the firstoccupier homesteading rule, as will be seen below.

Scarcity and Ideas

Like the magically-reproducible lawnmower, ideas are not scarce. If I invent a technique for harvesting cotton, your harvesting cotton in this way would not take away the technique from me. I still have my technique (as well as my cotton). Your use does not exclude my use; we could both use my technique to harvest cotton. There is no economic scarcity, and no possibility of conflict over the use of a scarce resource. Thus, there is no need for exclusivity.

Similarly, if you copy a book I have written, I still have the original (tangible) book, and I also still "have" the pattern of words that constitute the book. Thus, authored works are not scarce in the same sense that a piece of land or a car are scarce. If you take my car, I no longer have it. But if you "take" a book-pattern and use it to make your own physical book, I still have my own copy. The same holds true for inventions and, indeed, for any "pattern" or information one generates or has. As Thomas Jefferson—himself an inventor, as well as the first Patent Examiner in the U.S.—wrote, "He who receives an idea from me, receives instruction himself without lessening mine; as he who lights his taper at mine, receives light without darkening me."[62] Since use of another's idea does not deprive

---

[62]Thomas Jefferson to Isaac McPherson, Monticello, August 13, 1813, letter, in *The Writings of Thomas Jefferson*, vol. 13, ed. A.A. Lipscomb and A.E. Bergh (Washington, D.C.: Thomas Jefferson Memorial Association, 1904), pp. 326–38. Jefferson recognized that because ideas are not scarce, patent and copyright are not natural rights, and can be justified only, if at all, on the utilitarian grounds of promoting useful inventions and literary works (and, even then, they must be created by statute, since they are not natural rights). See Palmer, "Intellectual Property: A Non-Posnerian Law and Economics Approach," p. 278 n. 53. Yet this does not mean that Jefferson supported patents, even on utilitarian grounds. Patent historian Edward C. Walterscheid explains that "throughout his life, [Jefferson] retained a healthy skepticism

him of its use, no conflict over its use is possible; ideas, therefore, are not candidates for property rights. Even Rand acknowledged that "intellectual property cannot be consumed."[63]

Ideas are not naturally scarce. However, by recognizing a right in an ideal object, one *creates* scarcity where none existed before. As Arnold Plant explains:

> It is a peculiarity of property rights in patents (and copyrights) that they do not arise out of the scarcity of the objects which become appropriated. They are not a *consequence* of scarcity. They are the deliberate creation of statute law, and, whereas in general the institution of private property makes for the preservation of scarce goods, tending . . . to lead us "to make the most of them," property rights in patents and copyrights make possible the creation of a scarcity of the products appropriated which could not otherwise be maintained.[64]

---

about the value of the patents system." "Thomas Jefferson and the Patent Act of 1793," *Essays in History* 40 (1998).

[63]Rand, "Patents and Copyrights," p. 131. Mises, in *Human Action*, p. 661, recognizes that there is no need to economize in the employment of "formulas," "because their serviceableness cannot be exhausted." On p. 128, he points out:

> A thing rendering such unlimited services is, for instance, the knowledge of the causal relation implied. The formula, the recipe that teaches us how to prepare coffee, provided it is known, renders unlimited services. It does not lose anything from its capacity to produce however often it is used; its productive power is inexhaustible; it is therefore not an economic good. Acting man is never faced with a situation in which he must choose between the use-value of a known formula and any other useful thing.

See also p. 364.

[64]Plant, "The Economic Theory Concerning Patents for Inventions," p. 36. Also Mises, *Human Action*, p. 364: "Such recipes are, as a rule, free goods as their ability to produce definite effects is unlimited. They can become economic goods only if they are monopolized and their use is restricted. Any price paid for the services rendered by a recipe is always a monopoly price. It is immaterial whether the restriction of a recipe's use is made possible by institutional conditions—such as patents and copyright laws—or by the fact that a formula is kept secret and other people fail to guess it."

Bouckaert also argues that natural scarcity is what gives rise to the need for property rules, and that IP laws create an artificial, unjustifiable scarcity. As he notes:

> Natural scarcity is that which follows from the relationship between man and nature. Scarcity is natural when it is possible to conceive of it before any human, institutional, contractual arrangement. Artificial scarcity, on the other hand, is the outcome of such arrangements. Artificial scarcity can hardly serve as a justification for the legal framework that causes that scarcity. Such an argument would be completely circular. On the contrary, artificial scarcity itself needs a justification.[65]

Thus, Bouckaert maintains that "only naturally scarce entities over which physical control is possible are candidates for" protection by *real* property rights.[66] For ideal objects, the only protection possible is that achievable through *personal* rights, i.e., contract (more on this below).[67]

---

[65] Bouckaert, "What is Property?" p. 793; see also pp. 797–99.

[66] Bouckaert, "What is Property?" pp. 799, 803.

[67] It could also be argued that ideal objects deserve legal protection as property because they are "public goods," that is, because of negative externalities which arise if IP is not legally protected. However, the concept of public goods is neither coherent nor justifiable. See Palmer, "Intellectual Property: A Non-Posnerian Law and Economics Approach," pp. 279–80, 283–87; Hans-Hermann Hoppe, "Fallacies of the Public Goods Theory and the Production of Security," *Journal of Libertarian Studies* 9, no. 1 (Winter 1989): 27; also Hoppe, *The Economics and Ethics of Private Property*, chap. 1. As Palmer points out:

> the cost of producing any service or good includes not only labor, capital marketing, and other cost components, but also fencing (or exclusion) costs as well. Movie theaters, for example, invest in exclusion devices like ticket windows, walls, and ushers, all designed to exclude non-contributors from enjoyment of service. Alternatively, of course, movie owners could set up projectors and screens in public parks and then attempt to prevent passers-by from watching, or they could ask government to force all non-contributors to wear special glasses which prevent them from enjoying the movie. 'Drive-ins,' faced with the prospect of free riders peering over the walls, installed—at considerable expense—individual speakers for each car,

Only tangible, scarce resources are the possible object of interpersonal conflict, so it is only for them that property rules are applicable. Thus, patents and copyrights are unjustifiable monopolies granted by government legislation. It is not surprising that, as Palmer notes, "[m]onopoly privilege and censorship lie at the historical root of patent and copyright."[68] It is this monopoly privilege that creates an artificial scarcity where there was none before.

Let us recall that IP rights give to pattern-creators partial rights of control—ownership—over the tangible property of everyone else. The pattern-creator has partial ownership of others' property, by virtue of his IP right, because he can prohibit them from performing certain actions *with their own property*. Author X, for example, can prohibit a third party, Y, from inscribing a certain pattern of words on Y's own blank pages with Y's own ink.

That is, by merely authoring an original expression of ideas, by merely thinking of and recording some original *pattern* of information, or by finding a new way to use his own property (recipe), the IP creator instantly, magically becomes a partial owner of others' property. He has some say over how third parties can use their property. IP rights

---

thus rendering the publicly available visual part of the movie of little interest. . . . The costs of exclusion are involved in the production of virtually every good imaginable. There is no compelling justification for singling out some goods and insisting that the state underwrite their production costs through some sort of state-sanctioned collective action, simply because of a decision to make the good available on a nonexclusive basis.

Palmer, "Intellectual Property: A Non-Posnerian Law and Economics Approach," pp. 284–85. There is no way to show that ideas are clearly public goods. Moreover, even if ideas were public goods, this does not justify treating them as property rights, for the same reasons that even wealth-increasing measures are not necessarily justified, as discussed above.

[68]Palmer, "Intellectual Property: A Non-Posnerian Law and Economics Approach," p. 264.

change the *status quo* by redistributing property from individuals of one class (tangible-property owners) to individuals of another (authors and inventors). *Prima facie*, therefore, IP law trespasses against or "takes" the property of tangible property owners, by transferring partial ownership to authors and inventors. It is this invasion and redistribution of property that must be justified in order for IP rights to be valid. We see, then, that utilitarian defenses do not do the trick. Further problems with natural-rights defenses are explored below.

Creation vs. Scarcity

Some inconsistencies and problems with natural-rights theories of IP were pointed out above. This section discusses further problems with such arguments, in light of the preceding discussion of the significance of scarcity.

As noted before, some libertarian IP advocates, such as Rand, hold that *creation* is the source of property rights.[69] This confuses the nature and reasons for property rights, which lie in the undeniable fact of scarcity. *Given* scarcity and the correspondent possibility of conflict in the use of resources, conflicts are avoided and peace and cooperation are achieved by allocating property rights to such resources. And the purpose of property rights dictates the nature of such rules. For if the rules allocating property rights are to serve as objective rules that all can agree upon so as to avoid conflict, they cannot be biased or arbitrary.[70] For this reason, unowned resources come to be owned—homesteaded or appropriated—by the *first* possessor.[71]

---

[69]See Rand, "Patents and Copyrights"; Kelley, "Response to Kinsella"; Franck, "Intellectual and Personality Property" and "Intellectual Property Rights: Are Intangibles True Property?"

[70]See Hoppe, *A Theory of Socialism and Capitalism*, chap. 7, esp. p. 138.

[71]Hoppe, *A Theory of Socialism and Capitalism*, p. 142; de Jasay, *Against Politics*, pp. 172–79; and Herbener, "The Pareto Rule and Welfare Economics," p. 105.

The general rule, then, is that ownership of a given scarce resource can be identified by determining who first occupied it. There are various ways to possess or occupy resources, and different ways to demonstrate or prove such occupation, depending upon the nature of the resource and the use to which it is put. Thus, I can pluck an apple from the wild and thereby homestead it, or I can fence in a plot of land for a farm. It is sometimes said that one form of occupation is "forming" or "creating" the thing.[72] For example, I can sculpt a statue from a block of marble, or forge a sword from raw metal, or even "create" a farm on a plot of land.

We can see from these examples that creation is relevant to the question of ownership of a given "created" scarce resource, such as a statue, sword, or farm, only to the extent that the act of creation is an act of occupation, or is otherwise evidence of first occupation. However, "creation" itself does not justify ownership in things; it is neither necessary nor sufficient. One cannot *create* some possibly disputed scarce resource without first using the raw materials used to create the item. But these raw materials are scarce, and either I own them or I do not. If not, then I do not own the resulting product. If I own the inputs, then, by virtue of such ownership, I own the resulting thing into which I transform them.

Consider the forging of a sword. If I own some raw metal (because I mined it from ground I owned), then I own the same metal after I have shaped it into a sword. I do not need to rely on the fact of creation to own the sword, but only on my ownership of the factors used to make the sword.[73] And I do not need creation to come to

---

[72] Occupancy or taking possession "can take three forms: (1) by directly grasping it physically, (2) by forming it, and (3) by merely marking it as ours." Palmer, "Are Patents and Copyrights Morally Justified?" p. 838.

[73] I also do not need to rely on "ownership" of my labor; strictly speaking, labor cannot be owned, and labor ownership need not be relied on to show that I maintain ownership of my property as I transform it.

own the factors, since I can homestead them by simply mining them from the ground and thereby becoming the first possessor. On the other hand, if I fashion a sword using *your* metal, I do *not* own the resulting sword. In fact, I may owe you damages for trespass or conversion.

Creation, therefore, is neither necessary nor sufficient to establish ownership. The focus on creation distracts from the crucial role of first occupation as a property rule for addressing the fundamental fact of scarcity. First occupation, not creation or labor, is both necessary and sufficient for the homesteading of unowned scarce resources.

One reason for the undue stress placed on creation as the source of property rights may be the focus by some on *labor* as the means to homestead unowned resources. This is manifest in the argument that one homesteads unowned property with which one mixes one's labor *because* one "owns" one's labor. However, as Palmer correctly points out, "*occupancy, not labor*, is the act by which external things become property."[74] By focusing on first occupancy, rather than on labor, as the key to homesteading, there is no need to place creation as the fount of property rights, as Objectivists and others do. Instead, property rights must be recognized in first-comers (or their contractual transferees) in order to avoid the omnipresent problem of conflict over scarce resources. Creation itself is neither necessary nor sufficient to gain rights in unowned resources. Further, there is no need to maintain the strange view that one "owns" one's labor in order to own things one first occupies. Labor is a type of action, and action is not ownable; rather, it is the way that some tangible things (e.g., bodies) act in the world.

---

[74] Palmer, "Are Patents and Copyrights Morally Justified?" p. 838 (emphasis added), citing Georg W.F. Hegel, *Hegel's Philosophy of Right*, trans. T.M. Knox. (1821; reprint, London: Oxford University Press, 1967), pp. 45–46.

The problem with the natural rights defense of IP, then, lies in the argument that because an author-inventor "creates" some "thing," he is "thus" entitled to own it. The argument begs the question by assuming that the ideal object is ownable in the first place; once this is granted, it seems natural that the "creator" of this piece of property is the natural and proper owner of it. However, ideal objects are not ownable.

Under the libertarian approach, *when* there is a scarce (ownable) resource, we identify its owner by determining who its first occupier is. In the case of "created" goods (i.e., sculptures, farms, etc.), it can sometimes be assumed that the creator is also the first occupier by virtue of the gathering of raw materials and the very act of creation (imposing a pattern on the matter, fashioning it into an artifact, and the like). But it is not creation *per se* that gives rise to ownership, as pointed out above.[75] For similar reasons, the Lockean idea of "mixing labor" with a scarce resource is relevant only because it *indicates* that the user has possessed

---

[75] Even such advocates of IP as Rand do not maintain that creation *per se* is sufficient to give rise to rights, or that creation is even necessary. It is not necessary because unowned property can be homesteaded by simply occupying it, which involves no "creation" unless one stretches the concept without limit. It is also not sufficient, because Rand would certainly not hold that creating an item using raw material owned by *others* gives the thief-creator ownership of the item. Rand's view even implies that rights, including property rights, only arise when there is a possibility of conflict. Rand, for example, views rights as a social concept arising only when there is more than one person. See Rand, "Man's Rights," in *Capitalism: The Unknown Ideal*, p. 321: "A 'right' is a moral principle defining and sanctioning a man's freedom of action in a social context." Indeed, as Rand argues, "Man's rights can be violated only by the use of physical force," i.e., some conflict over a scarce resource. "The Nature of Government," in *Capitalism: The Unknown Ideal*, p. 330. On p. 334, Rand attempts (unsuccessfully) to justify government, the agent that enforces rights, based on the fact that there can be "honest disagreements"—i.e., conflict—even among "fully rational and faultlessly moral" men. So, in Rand's theory, creation *per se* is neither necessary nor sufficient, just as in the theory of property advocated herein.

the property (for property must be *possessed* in order to be labored upon). It is not because the labor must be rewarded, nor because we "own" labor and "therefore" its fruits. In other words, creation and labor-mixing *indicate* when one has occupied—and, thus, homesteaded— unowned scarce resources.[76]

---

[76]It is for these reasons that I disagree with the creation-centered approach of Objectivists David Kelley and Murray Franck. According to Franck, "Intellectual and Personality Property," p. 7, "although property rights help 'ration' scarcity, scarcity is not the basis of property rights. The view that it is . . . appears to reverse cause and effect in that it sees rights as a function of society's needs rather than as inherent in the individual who in turn must live in society."

I am not sure what it means to say that rights, which are relational concepts that only apply in a social context, are "inherent" in an individual, or that they are "functions" of anything. The former notion verges on the positivistic (in implying rights have a "source," as if they could be decreed by God or government), and the latter borders on the scientistic (in using the precise mathematical and natural-sciences notion of "functions"). And the argument for property rights is not based on a need to "ration" scarce items, but, instead, on the need of individuals to employ means to achieve ends, and to avoid interpersonal conflict over such means. Thus, scarcity is not the "basis" for property rights, but a necessary background condition that must obtain before property rights can arise or make sense; conflict can arise only over scarce resources, not abundant ones. (As pointed out in the preceding footnote, Objectivism also holds that conflict-possibility is just such a necessary condition for property rights.)

Moreover, the scarcity-based argument set forth here is no more a "function of society's needs" than is Franck's Objectivist approach. Franck believes that men "need" to be able to create things in order to survive—in a social setting where the presence of other men makes disputes possible. "Thus," law should protect rights to created things. But the scarcity-based argument recognizes that men "need" to be able to use scarce resources and that this requires conflicts to be avoided; thus, law should allocate property rights in scarce resources. Whatever the relative merits of the creation-based and the scarcity-based positions, the scarcity argument is not more collectivist than the creation argument, and the creation argument is not more individualist than the scarcity argument.

Kelley, in "Response to Kinsella," p. 13, writes:

> Property rights are required because man needs to support his life by the use of his reason. The primary task in this regard is to create values that satisfy human needs, rather than relying on what we find in nature, as animals do. . . . [T]he essential basis of property rights lies

By focusing on creation and labor, rather than on first occupancy of scarce resources, as the touchstone of property rights, IP advocates are led to place undue stress on the importance of "rewarding" the labor of the creator, much as Adam Smith's flawed labor theory of value led to Marx's even more deeply-flawed communist views on exploitation.[77] As noted above, for Rand, IP rights are, in a

---

in the phenomenon of creating value. . . . Scarcity becomes a relevant issue when we consider the use of things in nature, such as land, as inputs to the process of creating value. As a general rule, I would say that two conditions are required in order to appropriate things in nature and make them one's property: (1) one must put them to some productive use, and (2) that productive use must require exclusive control over them, i.e., the right to exclude others. . . . Condition (2) holds only when the resource is scarce. But for things that one has created, such as a new product, one's act of creation is the source of the right, regardless of scarcity." (emphasis added).

My reasons for disagreeing with Kelley here should be apparent, but let me point out that all human action, including creation of "values," has to rely on the use of scarce means, that is, the material stuff of the world. Each act of creation employs things made of already existing atoms; neither this fact, nor the recognition of it, is animal-like in any pejorative sense. That men, as opposed to animals, wish to create higher-order values by using scarce resources does not change this analysis. Second, Kelley advocates two separate rules for homesteading scarce resources: by first use of the resource, and by creating a new, useful, or artistic pattern with one's own property, which gives the creator the right to stop all others from using a similar pattern, even with their own property. As discussed below, these two homesteading rules are in conflict, and only the former can be justified. Finally, Kelley states that the creator of a new product owns it because he created it, regardless of scarcity. If Kelley here means a tangible product, such as a mousetrap, such a good is an actual, scarce, tangible thing. Presumably, the creator owned the scarce raw materials which he transformed into the final product. But he does not need to have a right in the ideal object of the mousetrap-idea or pattern in order to own the final product itself; he already owned the raw materials, and still owns them after he reshapes them. If Kelley instead means that, by creating a pattern or idea, one acquires the right of control over all others' scarce resources, then he is advocating a new type of homesteading rule, which I criticize below.

[77]See, e.g., Murray N. Rothbard, *Economic Thought Before Adam Smith: An Austrian Perspective on the History of Economic Thought*, vol. 1 (Brookfield, Vt.: Edward Elgar, 1995), p. 453: "It was, indeed, Adam Smith who was almost solely responsible for the injection into economics of the labour theory of value. And hence it was Smith who may plausibly be held responsible for the emergence and the

sense, the reward for productive work, i.e., *labor*. Rand and other natural-rights IP proponents seem to adopt a mixed natural rights—utilitarian rationale in holding that the person who invests time and effort must be rewarded or benefit from this effort (e.g., Rand opposed perpetual patent and copyright on the grounds that because distant descendants did not create their ancestors' works, they deserve no reward).[78]

In addition, in a strange admixture of natural-rights and utilitarian thinking, the natural-rights IP approach implies that something is property if it can hold *value*. But as Hoppe has trenchantly shown, one cannot have a property right in the *value* of one's property, but only in its physical integrity.[79] Moreover, many arbitrarily-defined "things" can acquire economic value if government grants a monopoly over the thing's use, even if the thing is not otherwise a scarce resource (e.g., the Postal Service's monopoly power to deliver first-class letters).

Thus, because ideas are not scarce resources in the sense that physical conflict over their use is possible, they are not the proper subject of property rights designed to avoid such conflicts.

---

momentous consequences of Marx." Even otherwise sound thinkers sometimes place undue stress on the importance of labor to the homesteading process and its ability to be "owned." Rothbard himself, for instance, implies that an individual "owns his own person and therefore *his own labor*." Rothbard, "Justice and Property Rights," p. 284, emphasis added; see also Rothbard, *The Ethics of Liberty*, p. 49. It is a misleading metaphor to speak of "owning one's labor" (or one's life or ideas). The right to use or profit from one's labor is only a *consequence* of being in control of one's body, just as the right to "free speech" is only a consequence, or a derivative, of the right to private property, as Rothbard recognized in *The Ethics of Liberty*, esp. chap. 15.

[78]See also Reisman, *Capitalism*, pp. 388–89.

[79]Hoppe, *A Theory of Socialism and Capitalism*, pp. 139–41, 237 n. 17.

Two Types of Homesteading

What, though, is really wrong with recognizing "new" property rights? After all, since new ideas, artistic creations, and innovations continually enrich us, what is the harm in moving with the times by recognizing new forms of property? The problem is that if property rights are recognized in non-scarce resources, this necessarily means that property rights in tangible resources are correspondingly diminished. This is because the only way to recognize ideal rights, in our real, scarce world, is to allocate rights in tangible goods. For me to have an effective patent right—a right in an idea or pattern, not in a scarce resource—means that I have some control over everyone else's scarce resources.

In fact, we can see that IP rights imply a new rule for acquiring rights in scarce resources, which undercuts the libertarian homesteading principle. For, according to Lockean-libertarian homesteading, it is the *first occupier* of a previously unowned scarce resource who homesteads it, i.e., becomes its owner. A late-comer who seizes control of all or part of such owned property is simply a thief, because the property is already owned. The thief effectively proposes a new and arbitrary homesteading rule to replace the first-occupier rule, namely, the particularistic rule "I become the owner of property when I forcibly take it from you." Of course, such a rule is no rule at all, and is clearly inferior to the first-possessor rule. The thief's rule is particular, not universal; it is not just, and it certainly is not designed to avoid conflicts.

Proponents of IP must also advocate a new homesteading rule to supplement, if not replace, the first-possessor homesteading rule. They must maintain that there is a *second* way for an individual to come to own tangible property. To wit, the IP advocate must propose some homesteading rule along the following lines: "A person who comes up with some useful or creative idea which can guide or direct an actor in the *use* of his own tangible property thereby instantly gains a right to control all other tangible property in the world, with respect to that property's similar use." This new-fangled homesteading technique is so powerful that it gives the creator rights in third parties' *already owned* tangible property.

For example, by inventing a new technique for digging a well, the inventor can prevent *all others* in the world from digging wells in this manner, *even on their own property*. To take another example, imagine the time when men lived in caves. One bright guy—let's call him Galt-Magnon—decides to build a log cabin on an open field, near his crops. To be sure, this is a good idea, and others notice it. They naturally imitate Galt-Magnon, and they start building their own cabins. But the first man to invent a house, according to IP advocates, would have a right to prevent others from building houses on their own land, with their own logs, or to charge them a fee if they do build houses. It is plain that the innovator in these examples becomes a *partial owner* of the tangible property (e.g., land and logs) of others, due *not* to first occupation and use of that property (for it is already owned), but due to his *coming up with an idea*. Clearly, this rule flies in the face of the first-user homesteading rule, arbitrarily and groundlessly overriding the very homesteading rule that is at the foundation of all property rights.

There is, in fact, no reason why merely innovating gives the innovator partial ownership of property that others already own. Just because a rule can be proposed does not mean that it is workable or just. There are many arbitrary rules one could dream up by which property rights could be allocated. For example, a racist could propose that any white person can homestead any property already first homesteaded by a black person. Or: the *third* occupier of a scarce resource becomes its owner. Or: the state can homestead all capital goods, even if already first acquired by individuals. Or: by legislative decree, the state can homestead, in the form of taxes, part of the estates that are already owned by private individuals. All such arbitrary homesteading rules, including the IP rule that innovators homestead partial control of all others' tangible resources, are unjustifiable. They all conflict with the only justifiable homesteading rule, *first occupation*. None of them establish fair, objective rules that avoid interpersonal conflict over scarce resources. Discussions of protecting rights in "ideas," "creations," or "things of value" only serves to obscure the fact that the proponent of IP opposes the unadulterated right to homestead and own private property.

IP AS CONTRACT

The Limits of Contract

The law, then, should protect individual rights to one's body, and to legitimately acquired scarce resources (property). There is not a natural right to ideal objects—to one's intellectual innovations or creations—but only to scarce resources. Many opponents of IP rights typically support only *contractual* arrangements to protect ideas and innovations—private contracts between property owners.[80] Suppose, for example, that A writes a book and sells physical copies of it to numerous purchasers B_1, B_2 ... B_N, with a contractual condition that each buyer B is obligated not to make or sell a copy of the text. Under all theories of contract, any

---

[80]See McElroy, "Intellectual Property: Copyright and Patent"; Roy Halliday, "Ideas as Property," *Formulations* 4, no. 4 (Summer 1997); Bouckaert, "What is Property?" pp. 804–5; Palmer, "Intellectual Property: A Non-Posnerian Law and Economics Approach," pp. 280, 291–95; Palmer, "Are Patents and Copyrights Morally Justified?" pp. 821 n. 8, 851–55, 864; and Richard O. Hammer, "Intellectual Property Rights Viewed as Contracts," *Formulations* 3, no. 2 (Winter 1995–96).

of the buyers *B* becomes liable to *A*, at least for damages, if he violates these provisions.[81]

But the advocates of the contractual approach to IP are mistaken if they believe that private contract can be used to recreate the same type of protection afforded by modern IP rights. Patent and copyright are good against *all* third parties, regardless of their consent to a contract. They are *real* rights that bind everyone, in the same way that my title to a parcel of land binds *everyone* to respect my property—even if they do not have a contract with me. A contract, by contrast, binds *only* parties to the contract. It is like private law between the parties.[82] It does not bind third parties, i.e., those not in "privity" with the original parties.[83]

Thus, if the book purchaser *B* relates to third parties *T* the plot of the purchased novel, these third parties *T* are not bound, in general, by the original contractual obligation between *A* and *B*. If I learn how to adjust my car's carburetor to double its efficiency, or if I learn of a poem or movie plot someone else has written, why should I have to pretend that I am ignorant of these things, and refrain from acting on this knowledge? I have not obligated myself by contract to the creator. I do not deny that contractual obligations can be implicit or tacit, but there is not even an implicit contract in such situations.

---

[81] See, e.g., Kinsella, "A Theory of Contracts"; Rothbard, *The Ethics of Liberty*, chap. 19; Williamson M. Evers, "Toward a Reformulation of the Law of Contracts," *Journal of Libertarian Studies* 1, no. 1 (Winter 1977): 3–13; and Randy E. Barnett, "A Consent Theory of Contract," *Columbia Law Review* 86 (1986): 269–321.

[82] Under the international law meta-rule *pacta sunt servanda* (contracts are to be observed), contracts between sovereigns (states, in the international law context) create a "law of the agreement" between the parties. See Paul E. Comeaux and N. Stephan Kinsella, *Protecting Foreign Investment Under International Law: Legal Aspects of Political Risk* (Dobbs Ferry, N.Y.: Oceana Publications, 1997), chaps. 2, 5.

[83] For a definition of "privity of contract," see *Black's Law Dictionary*, 6th ed. (St. Paul, Minn.: West Publishing, 1990), p. 1199. See also, in the IP context, Bouckaert, "What is Property?" pp. 795, 805.

Nor can it be said as a general matter that I have stolen or fraudulently acquired the information, as there are many legitimate ways for individuals to acquire information. Artistic works, by their very nature, typically are made public. Scientific discoveries and innovations likewise can become known beyond the parties to confidentiality agreements. And it certainly cannot be said that my use of my carburetor, or writing a novel using the same plot, physically interferes with the creator's use of his own tangible property. It does not even prevent the creator from using his own carburetor idea to improve his own car or others', or from using that plot.

So, my adjusting my carburetor is not a breach of contract; it is not theft; and it is not physical trespass on the inventor's tangible property. Twiddling my carburetor does not violate the inventor's rights. At most, my use of this idea will diminish its *value* to the inventor by hampering his ability to monopolistically exploit it. As we have seen, however, one cannot have a right to the value of one's property, but only in its physical integrity.[84]

Thus, the use of contract only gets us so far. A book publisher may be able to contractually obligate his purchasers to not copy his book, but he cannot prevent third parties from publishing and selling it, unless some contract prohibits this action.

Contract vs. Reserved Rights

Third parties, then, who are not parties to the contract and are not in privity with the contractual obligor and obligee, are not bound by the contractual relationship. For this reason, although an innovator can use contract to stop specified individuals from freely using his ideas, it is difficult to use standard contract law to prevent third parties from using ideas they glean from others. Perhaps sensing

---

[84]Hoppe, *A Theory of Socialism and Capitalism*, pp. 139–41, 237 n. 17.

this problem, some quasi-IP advocates shift from a purely contractual approach to a "reservation of rights" approach in which property rights in tangible resources are seen as a divisible bundle of rights.

For example, under the standard bundle-of-rights view, a landowner can sell the mineral estate to an oil company while retaining all rights to the surface, except for an easement (servitude) granting passage to a neighbor and a life estate (usufruct) granting use of the surface estate to his mother. Drawing on the bundle-of-rights notion, the "reservation of rights" approach holds that a type of "private" IP can be privately generated by creatively "reserving rights" to *reproduce* tangible items sold to purchasers.

Rothbard, for example, argues that one can grant conditional "ownership" (of "knowledge") to another, while "retaining the ownership power to disseminate the knowledge of the invention." Or, Brown, the inventor of an improved mousetrap, can stamp it "copyright" and thereby sell the right to each mousetrap *except for* the right to reproduce it. Like the real rights accompanying statutory IP, such "reservations" allegedly bind everyone, not just those who have contracted with the original seller. Thus, third parties who become aware of, purchase, or otherwise come into possession of the restricted item also cannot reproduce it—*not* because they have entered into a contract with Brown, but because "no one can acquire a *greater* property title in something than has already been given away or sold." In other words, the third party acquires a tangible thing—a book or a mousetrap, say—but it is somehow "missing" the "right-to-copy" part of the bundle of rights that "normally" constitutes all rights to the thing. Or, the third party acquires "ownership" of information, from a person who did not own the information and, thus, was not entitled to transmit it to others.[85]

---

[85] Rothbard, *The Ethics of Liberty*, p. 123.

But surely something is amiss here. Suppose that A writes a novel and sells a first copy, $BOOK_1$, without restriction (i.e., without a reservation of rights) to B_1; and a second copy, $BOOK_2$, to B_2—but "reserving" the book's inherent "right to copy." The two books, $BOOK_1$ and $BOOK_2$, appear to third parties to be otherwise identical. Yet they are not: one is incomplete; the other somehow contains more mystical "rights-essence" within its covers. Suppose B_1 and B_2 leave these books on a park bench, where they are discovered by third party T. According to Rothbard, $BOOK_2$ is "missing" the "right to copy," much like an electronic toy that is sold "batteries not included." It is as if there is an invisible, mystical tendril of "reproduction-ownership" stretching from $BOOK_2$ back to its true owner A, wherever he may be. Thus, even if T finds and homesteads the abandoned $BOOK_2$, this book simply does not contain "within itself" the right to permit the owner to copy it. It is being continually siphoned away by a rights wormhole which connects the item to owner A. Thus, if T homesteads the book, he still homesteads no more than he acquires. T homesteads only a book without a right to copy "built in," and, thus, does not have the right to copy $BOOK_2$. The same is true for subsequent third parties who come to possess the book.

Is such a view really tenable? Can we conceive of property rights working this way? Even if we can, would it really achieve the desired result here—preventing third parties from using the protected ideas? It is difficult to maintain that rights can be reserved in this manner. One function of property rights, after all, is to prevent conflict and to put third parties *on notice* as to the property's boundaries. The borders of property must necessarily be objective and intersubjectively ascertainable; they must be *visible*. Only if borders are visible *can* they be respected and property rights serve their function of permitting conflict-avoidance. Only if these borders are both visible and objectively just (justifiable in discourse) can they be expected to be adopted and followed. But think of the two books, BOOK$_1$ and BOOK$_2$. How could one tell the difference between them? How could one see the rights-tendril connected to the latter but not to the former? How can third parties be expected to respect an amorphous, invisible, mystical, spooky, possibly unknown and unknowable property border?

The implications of such a view are troubling. Palmer writes:

> The separation and retention of the right to copy from the bundle of rights that we call property is problematic. Could one reserve the right, for example, to remember something? Suppose that I wrote a book and offered it to you to read, but I had retained one right: the right to remember it. Would I be justified in taking you to court if I could prove that you had remembered the name of the lead character in the book?[86]

---

[86]Palmer, "Are Patents and Copyrights Morally Justified?" p. 853. Palmer also quotes the following illuminating passages.

Hegel argued:

> The substance of an author's or an inventor's right cannot in the first instance be found in the supposition that when he disposes of a single copy of his work, he arbitrarily makes it a condition that the power to produce facsimiles as things, a power which thereupon passes into another's possession, should not become the property of the other but should remain his own. The first question is whether such a separation between ownership of the thing and the power to produce facsimiles which is given with the thing is compatible with the concept of property, or whether it does not cancel the complete and free ownership on which there originally depends the option of the single producer of intellectual work to reserve to himself the power to reproduce, or to part with this power as a thing of value, or to attach no value to it at all and surrender it together with the single exemplar of his work. (*Hegel's Philosophy of Right*, p. 55, quoted in Palmer, "Are Patents and Copyrights Morally Justified?" p. 853 n. 138)

And, as Kant noted:

> Those who regard the publication of a book as the exercise of the rights of property in respect of a single copy—it may have come to

But third parties still pose a problem for this theory. Even if a seller of an object could somehow "reserve" certain use-rights with respect to the sold object, how does this prevent third parties from using *information* apparent from or conveyed in that object? Reserved rights proponents say *more* than that the immediate buyer B_1 is bound not to reproduce the book; for this result could be obtained by pointing to the implicit *contract* between seller A and buyer B_1. Let us consider a third party, T_1, who finds and reads the abandoned book, thus *learning* the information in it. Alternatively, consider third party T_2, who never has possession of or even sees the book; he merely learns of the information in the book from gossip, graffiti, unsolicited e-mail, and so forth. Neither T_1 nor T_2 has a contract with A, but both now possess certain knowledge. Even if the book somehow does not contain within it a "right to reproduce," how can this prevent T_1 and T_2 from using their own knowledge? And even if we say that T_1 is somehow "bound" by a contractual copyright notice printed on the book (an untenable view of contract), how is T_2 bound by any contract or reserved right?

Rothbard attempts to address this point as follows:

---

the possessor as a [manuscript] of the author, or as a work printed by some prior publisher—and who yet would, by the reservation of certain rights, . . . go on to restrict the exercise of property rights, maintaining the illegality of reproduction—will never attain their end. For the rights of an author regarding his own thoughts remain to him notwithstanding the reprint; and as there cannot be a distinct permission given to the purchaser of a book for, and a limitation of, its use as property, how much less is a mere presumption sufficient for such a weight of obligation? (Immanuel Kant, "Was ist ein Buch?" in *Die Metaphysic die Sitten*, ed. W. Weischedel [Frankfurt a.M.: Suhrkamp Verlag, 1977], p. 581, translated and quoted in Palmer, "Are Patents and Copyrights Morally Justified?" p. 853 n. 138)

For an alternative translation, see Immanuel Kant, *Essay Three: Of the Injustice of Counterfeiting Books*, trans. John Richardson, ed. and rev. Stephen Palmquist (Philopsychy Press, 1994).

> A common objection runs as follows: all right, it would be criminal for *Green* [the buyer] to produce and sell the Brown mousetrap; but suppose that someone else, Black, who had not made a contract with Brown, happens to see Green's mousetrap and then goes ahead and produces and sells the replica? Why should *he* be prosecuted? The answer is that . . . no one can acquire a *greater* property title in something than has already been given away or sold. Green did not own the total property right in his mousetrap, in accordance with his contract with Brown—but only all rights *except* to sell . . . a replica. But therefore Black's title in the mousetrap, the ownership of the ideas in Black's head, can be no greater than Green's, and therefore he too would be a violator of Brown's property even though he himself had not made the actual contract.[87]

There are several problems with this reasoning. First of all, Black merely *sees* Green's mousetrap. He does not see or have access to ideas in Green's head. Nor does he need to have such access in order to duplicate evident features of the mousetrap.

Further, ideas in one's head are not "owned" any more than labor is owned. Only scarce resources are owned. By losing sight of scarcity as a necessary aspect of a homesteadable thing, and of the first occupancy homesteading rule as the way to own such things, Rothbard and others are sidetracked into the mistaken notion that ideas and labor can be owned. If we recognize that ideas cannot be owned (they are not scarce resources), that creation is neither necessary nor sufficient for ownership (first occupancy is), and that labor need not be "owned" in order to be a homesteader, then the trouble caused by these confused notions disappears.

---

[87] Rothbard, *The Ethics of Liberty*, p. 123.

If Black *somehow* comes into possession of the ideas implicit in an item which Brown invented (in Rothbard's example, he "happens to see" it), it is *irrelevant* that the mousetrap may not have had a "right to copy" built into it. For Black does not need such permission to use his own property as he sees fit. How does "happening to see" the mousetrap make Black a trespasser or violator of Brown's rights?

All action, including action which employs owned scarce means (property), involves the use of technical knowledge.[88] Some of this knowledge may be gained from things we see, including the property of others. We do not have to have a "right to copy" as part of a bundle of rights to have a right to impose a known pattern or form on an object we own. Rather, we have a right to do *anything at all* with and on our own property, provided *only* that we do not invade others' property borders. We must not lose sight of this crucial libertarian point. If I own a 100-acres of land, I can prance around naked on it, *not* because the land is imbued with some "right-to-prance-naked," but because I *own* the land and it does not (necessarily) violate the property rights of others for me to use my property in this fashion.

Similarly, I am entitled to do what I want with my own property—my car, my paper, my word processor—including improving my car's carburetor or using my ink to print words on my paper. That is, *unless* I have contractually obligated myself to someone else to restrict my actions with respect to my use of this knowledge. I do not have to first find in my property a right-to-use-in-a-certain-way, for all ways of using it, *except* those that cause invasions of others' property borders, are already encompassed within the general *right to use* my property. In libertarianism, we live by

---

[88]Kinsella, "Knowledge, Calculation, Conflict, and Law"; Jörg Guido Hülsmann, "Knowledge, Judgment, and the Use of Property," *Review of Austrian Economics* 10, no. 1 (1997), p. 44.

right, not permission. We do not need to find permission to take actions with our own property. Contrary to practice in totalitarian societies, all things that are not forbidden are permitted. The reservation-of-rights view would reverse this by assuming that every use of property is valid only if that particular use-right can be somehow found or located in the property.

Consider the following analogy. Farmer Jed discovers oil under his land. No one for miles around knows about the black gold. Jed plans to buy his neighbors' property for a song; they'll sell it cheap, too, since they don't know about the oil. In the middle of the night, his nosy neighbor Cooter, suspicious over Jed's recent good spirits, sneaks onto Jed's land and discovers the truth. The next morning, at Floyd's barbershop, Cooter spills his guts to Clem and the boys. One of them promptly runs to a pay phone and gives a tip to a reporter at the *Wall Street Journal* (who happens to be his nephew). Soon, it is common knowledge that there is oil in the vicinity. The neighbors now demand exorbitant prices for their land, thus spoiling Jed's plans.

Let us grant that Cooter can be prosecuted for trespass and harms flowing therefrom. The question is, can Jed's neighbors be prevented from acting on their knowledge? That is, may they be forced to somehow *pretend* that they do not know about the oil, and sell their land to Jed for what they "would have" sold it when in ignorance? Of course they may not be so forced. They own their land, and are entitled to use it as they see fit. Unlike tangible property, information is not ownable; it is not property. The possessor of a stolen watch may have to return it, but so long as the acquirer of knowledge does not obtain that knowledge illicitly or in violation of a contract, he is free to act upon it.

Note, however, that according to the reservation-of-rights view, the neighbors would not be permitted to act upon their knowledge because they obtained it ultimately from Cooter, a trespasser who had no "title" to that knowledge. Thus, they could not have obtained "greater title" to it than Cooter himself had. Note also that others, such as geological surveyors mapping oil deposits, cannot include this information in their maps. They must feign ignorance until given permission by Jed. This imposed ignorance correlates with the unnatural scarcity imposed by IP. There is clearly no warrant for the view that reserved rights can somehow prohibit third parties from using knowledge they acquire.

It is simply not legitimate to restrict the use to which an owner of property can put it unless that owner has contractually obligated himself or has otherwise acquired the information by a violation of the information-holder's rights. Talk of reserving the right to copy is merely a way to avoid the contractual notion that only parties to a contract are bound by it.[89]

Therefore, as a general matter, purchasers can be bound by contracts with sellers to not copy or even re-sell the thing. However, once third parties become aware of the ideas underlying the invention or literary work, their use of that knowledge does not, in general, violate any recognizable property rights of the seller.

Given this view of scarcity, property, and contract, let us examine the legitimacy of common forms of IP.

Copyright and Patent

As should be apparent, copyright and patent seek to prevent the owners of tangible property—scarce resources—from using their own property as they see fit. For example,

---

[89] Of course, in anarcho-capitalism, it is difficult to predict what extensive contractual regimes, networks, and institutions will arise. Various enclaves or communities may well require their customers, patrons, or "citizens" to abide by certain IP-like rules. On anarcho-capitalism, see, e.g., Hans-Hermann Hoppe, "The Private Production of Defense," *Journal of Libertarian Studies* 14, no. 1 (Winter 1998–1999): 27–52.

they are prohibited, under patent law, from practicing patented methods, using their own property, or from shaping their own property into patented devices, even if they independently invent the method or device. Under copyright law, third parties who have not contracted with the author are prevented from copying or profiting from the author's original work. Clearly, sellers of novel devices or literary works can contract with buyers to prevent these buyers from reproducing, or even re-selling, the item. These contractual webs can be elaborate; a novel writer can license his story to a movie studio on the condition that the studio require all movie theaters to require customers to agree not to reproduce the plot of the movie, and so on.

Yet, once third parties not bound by a contract acquire this information, they are free to use it as they see fit. The reserved-rights approach does not change this. Thus, it would probably be difficult to maintain anything similar to our present patent and copyright laws using contract alone.

Trade Secrets

Trade secrets are easier to justify than patent or copyright. Palmer argues that they "emerge" from common law-type rights, and are, thus, legitimate.[90] Trade secret law allows damages to be obtained for, or an injunction to be issued to prevent, acts of "misappropriation" of a trade secret. This can be applied against the person who has improperly acquired the trade secret or who divulges the secret contrary to a contractual obligation, and also against others who know that they are obtaining the secret from such a person.[91]

---

[90]Palmer, "Intellectual Property: A Non-Posnerian Law and Economics Approach," pp. 280, 292–93; and Palmer, "Are Patents and Copyrights Morally Justified?" pp. 854–55.
[91]UTSA, § 1; Halligan, "Restatement of the Third Law—Unfair Competition: A Brief Summary," § 40, comment d.

Suppose employee *A* of company *X* has access to *X*'s trade secrets, such as its secret formula for a soft drink. He is subject to an employment agreement obligating him to keep this formula secret. He then jumps to *X*'s competitor, *Y*. *Y* wants to use the formula it learns from *A* to compete with *X*. Under current law, so long as the secret formula has not been made public, *X* can get a court order to stop *A* from revealing the secret to *Y*. If *A* has already revealed the secret to *Y*, *X* can also get an injunction to stop *Y* from using or publicizing the formula.

Clearly, the injunction and damages against *A* are proper because *A* is in violation of his contract with *X*. More questionable is the injunction against *Y*, because Y had no contract with *X*. In the context in which such situations usually arise, however, where the competitor *Y* wants the trade secret and knows the defecting employee is in breach of contract, it could be argued that the competitor *Y* is acting in conspiracy with or as an accomplice of employee *A* to violate the (contractual) rights of trade secret holder *X*. This is because *A* has not actually breached his trade secrecy agreement until he reveals trade secrets to *Y*. If *Y* actively solicits *A* to do this, then *Y* is an accomplice or co-conspirator in the violation of *X*'s rights. Thus, just as the driver of the getaway car in a bank robbery, or the mafia boss who orders an assassination, are properly held liable for acts of aggression committed by others with whom they conspire, third parties can, in narrowly defined cases, be prevented from using a trade secret obtained from the trade secret thief.[92]

---

[92] On responsibility for conduct of another or for conspiracy, see, e.g., Texas Penal Code, §§ 7.02 (Criminal Responsibility for Conduct of Another), and 15.02 (criminal conspiracy). For definitions of "abet," "accessory," "accomplice," "aid and abet," "concert," and "conspiracy," see *Black's Law Dictionary*.

Trademarks

Palmer also argues that trademark law is legitimate.[93] Suppose some Lachmannian changes the name on his failing hamburger chain from LachmannBurgers to Rothbard Burgers, which is already the name of another hamburger chain. I, as a consumer, am hungry for a RothbardBurger. I see one of the fake RothbardBurger joints run by the stealthy Lachmannian, and I buy a burger. Under current law, Rothbard, the "owner" of the RothbardBurgers trademark, can prevent the Lachmannian from using the mark RothbardBurgers to sell burgers because it is "confusingly similar" to his own trademark. That is, it is likely to mislead consumers as to the true source of the goods purchased. The law, then, gives a right to the trademark holder against the trademark infringer.

In my view, it is the *consumers* whose rights are violated, not the trademark holder's. In the foregoing example, I (the consumer) thought I was buying a RothbardBurger, but instead got a crummy LachmannBurger with its weird kaleidoscopic sauce. I should have a right to sue the Lachmannian for fraud and breach of contract (not to mention intentional infliction of emotional distress and misrepresentation of praxeological truths). However, it is difficult to see how this act of fraud, perpetrated by the Lachmannian on *me*, violates *Rothbard*'s rights. The Lachmannian's actions do not physically invade Rothbard's property. He does not even convince others to do this; at most, he may be said to convince third parties to take an action within their rights, namely, to buy a burger from the Lachmannian instead of Rothbard. Thus, it would appear that, under libertarianism, trademark law should give *consumers*, not trademark *users*, the right to sue trademark pirates.

---

[93]Palmer, "Intellectual Property: A Non-Posnerian Law and Economics Approach," p. 280.

Moreover, more novel extensions of trademark, such as rights against trademark dilution or against certain forms of cybersquatting, cannot be justified. Just as a trademark holder does not have a right to his mark, neither does he have a right against his mark's dilution. The law against cybersquatting is simply based on an economically ignorant opposition to "scalping" and arbitrage. There is, of course, nothing wrong with being the first to acquire a domain name and thereafter selling it to the highest bidder.

CONCLUSION

We see, then, that a system of property rights in "ideal objects" necessarily requires violation of other individual property rights, e.g., to use one's own tangible property as one sees fit.[94] Such a system requires a new homesteading rule which subverts the firstoccupier rule. IP, at least in the form of patent and copyright, cannot be justified.

It is not surprising that IP attorneys, artists, and inventors often seem to take for granted the legitimacy of IP. However, those more concerned with liberty, truth, and rights should not take for granted the institutionalized use of force used to enforce IP rights. Instead, we should reassert the primacy of individual rights over our bodies and homesteaded scarce resources.

---

[94]See Palmer, "Intellectual Property: A Non-Posnerian Law and Economics Approach," p. 281; and Palmer, "Are Patents and Copyrights Morally Justified?" pp. 831, 862, 864–65.

Appendix

Some Questionable Examples of Patents and Copyrights

Some exemplary U.S. patents:[95]

- "Christmas Tree Stand Watering System," U.S. Pat. No. 4,993,176, Feb. 19, 1991 (Christmas tree watering stand shaped like Santa Claus);

- "Initiation Apparatus," U.S. Pat. No. 819,814, May 8, 1906 ("harmless" way of initiating a candidate into a fraternity by shocking him with electrodes);

- "Method of Exercising a Cat," U.S. Pat. No. 5,443,036, Aug. 22, 1995 (shining a laser light onto the floor to fascinate a cat and cause it to chase the light);

- "Pat on the Back Apparatus," U.S. Pat. No. 4,608,967, Sep. 2, 1986 (apparatus with simulated human hand to pat the user on the back);

- "Hyper-Light-Speed Antenna," U.S. Pat. No. 6,025,810, Feb. 15, 2000 (poking hole in another "dimension" to transmit RF waves at faster-than-light speed, incidentally accelerating plant growth);

- "Force-Sensitive, Sound-Playing Condom," U.S. Pat. No. 5,163,447, Nov. 17, 1992 (self-explanatory; for example, it could play "Dixie");

---

[95]These and other patents may be retrieved at http://www.delphion.com, http://www.uspto.gov/patft/index.html, or http://www.patentgopher.com. See also "Wacky Patent of the Month," http://colitz.com/site/wacky.htm; IBM, "Gallery of Obscure Patents," http://www.patents.ibm.com/gallery; and Greg Aharonian, "Bustpatents," http://www.bustpatents.com.

- "Method and System for Placing a Purchase Order via a Communications Network," U.S. Pat. No. 5,960,411, Sep. 28, 1999 (Amazon.com's "one-click" method for purchasing an item on the world wide web by single mouse-click);

- "Financial Certificates, System and Process," U.S. Pat. No. 6,017,063, Jan. 25, 2000 (inflation-indexed gift certificate or mutual fund share);

- "Method and System for Measuring Leadership Effectiveness," U.S. Pat. No. 6,007,340, Dec. 28, 1999 (assigned to Electronic Data Systems Corporation);

- "Sanitary Appliance for Birds," U.S. Pat. No. 2,882,858, April 21, 1959 (bird diaper);

- "Religious Soap," U.S. Pat. No. 3,936,384, Feb. 3, 1976 (bar of soap with religious design on one side and prayer on the other); and

- "Method of Preserving the Dead," U.S. Pat. No. 748,284, Dec. 29, 1903 (preserving dead person's head in block of glass).

Copyright law, while it has not led to as many clearly absurd applications, has also been extended greatly by the courts. Originally intended to cover literary works, the concept has been stretched so that authored "works" include computer programs, and even machine language and object code, which is more analogous to a machine part, such as a cam, than to a literary work.[96]

---

[96] *Final Report, National Commission on New Technological Uses (CONTU) of Copyright Works,* July 31, 1978 (Washington, D.C.: Library of Congress, 1979); *Apple Computer, Inc. v Franklin Computer Corporation,* 714 F2d 1240 (3d Cir 1983); *NEC Corp. and NEC Electronics, Inc. v Intel Corp.,* 1989 Copr.L.Dec. ¶ 26,379, 1989 WL 67434 (ND Cal 1989).

BIBLIOGRAPHY

Aharonian, Greg. "Bustpatents." http://www.bustpatents.com.

Barnett, Randy E. "A Consent Theory of Contract." *Columbia Law Review* 86 (1986): 269–321.

———. *The Structure of Liberty: Justice and The Rule of Law.* New York: Oxford University (Clarendon) Press, 1998.

"Bibliography of General Theories of Intellectual Property." *Encyclopedia of Law and Economics,* http://encyclo.findlaw.com/biblio/1600.htm.

Binswanger, Harry, ed. *The Ayn Rand Lexicon: Objectivism from A to Z.* New York: New American Library, 1986.

Black's Law Dictionary. 6th ed. St. Paul, Minn.: West Publishing, 1990.

Block, Walter. *Defending the Undefendable.* New York: Fleet Press, 1976.

———. "A Libertarian Theory of Blackmail." *Irish Jurist* 33 (1998): 280–310.

———. "Toward a Libertarian Theory of Blackmail." *Journal of Libertarian Studies* 15, no. 2 (Spring 2001).

———. "Toward a Libertarian Theory of Inalienability: A Critique of Rothbard, Barnett, Gordon, Smith, Kinsella and Epstein." *Journal of Libertarian Studies* 17, no. 2 (Spring 2003): 39–85.

Bouckaert, Boudewijn. "What is Property?" In "Symposium: Intellectual Property." *Harvard Journal of Law & Public Policy* 13, no. 3 (Summer 1990).

Breyer, Stephen. "The Uneasy Case for Copyright: A Study of Copyright in Books, Photocopies, and Computer Programs." *Harvard Law Review* 84 (1970).

Chisum, Donald S. *Chisum on Patents*. New York: Matthew Bender, 2000.

Cole, Julio H. "Patents and Copyrights: Do the Benefits Exceed the Costs?" http://www.economia.ufm.edu.gt/Catedraticos/jhcole/Cole%20_MPS_.pdf

Comeaux, Paul E., and N. Stephan Kinsella. *Protecting Foreign Investment Under International Law: Legal Aspects of Political Risk*. Dobbs Ferry, N.Y.: Oceana Publications, 1997.

Epstein, Richard. "Blackmail, Inc." *University of Chicago Law Review* 50 (1983).

Evers, Williamson M. "Toward a Reformulation of the Law of Contracts." *Journal of Libertarian Studies* 1, no. 1 (Winter 1977): 3–13.

Foerster, Stephen. "The Basics of Economic Government." http://www.economic.net/articles/ar0001.html.

Franck, Murray I. "Ayn Rand, Intellectual Property Rights, and Human Liberty." 2 audio tapes, Institute for Objectivist Studies Lecture (1991).

———. "Intellectual Property Rights: Are Intangibles True Property?" *IOS Journal* 5, no. 1 (April 1995).

———. "Intellectual and Personality Property." *IOS Journal* 5, no. 3 (September 1995).

Franklin Pierce Law Center. "Intellectual Property Mall." http://www.ipmall.fplc.edu.

Free World Order. "Invention and Intellectual Property." http://www.buildfreedom.com/ft/intellectual_property.htm.

Friedman, David D. "Standards As Intellectual Property: An Economic Approach." *University of Dayton Law Review* 19, no. 3 (Spring 1994): 1109–29.

———. "In Defense of Private Orderings: Comments on Julie Cohen's 'Copyright and the Jurisprudence of Self-Help'." *Berkeley Technology Law Journal* 13, no. 3 (Fall 1998): 1152–71.

———. *Law's Order: What Economics Has to do with Law and Why it Matters*. Princeton, N.J.: Princeton University Press, 2000.

Frost, Robert. "The Mending Wall." In *North of Boston*, 2nd ed. New York: Henry Holt, 1915.

Galambos, Andrew J. *The Theory of Volition*. Vol. 1. Edited by Peter N. Sisco. San Diego: Universal Scientific Publications, 1999.

Ginsburg, Jane C. "Copyright, Common Law, and *Sui Generis* Protection of Databases in the United States and Abroad." *University of Cincinnati Law Review* 66 (1997).

Goldstein, Paul. *Copyright: Principles, Law, and Practice*. Boston: Little, Brown, 1989.

Gordon, Wendy J. "An Inquiry into the Merits of Copyright: The Challenges of Consistency, Consent, and Encouragement Theory." *Stanford Law Review* 41 (1989).

Halliday, Roy. "Ideas as Property." *Formulations* 4, no. 4 (Summer 1997).

Hammer, Richard O. "Intellectual Property Rights Viewed as Contracts." *Formulations* 3, no. 2 (Winter 1995–96).

Hayek, F.A. *The Collected Works of F.A. Hayek*. Vol. 1, *Fatal Conceit: The Errors of Socialism*. Edited by W.W. Bartley. Chicago: University of Chicago Press, 1989.

Hegel, Georg W.F. *Hegel's Philosophy of Right*. Translated by T.M. Knox. 1821; reprint, London: Oxford University Press, 1967.

Herbener, Jeffrey M. "The Pareto Rule and Welfare Economics." *Review of Austrian Economics* 10, no. 1 (1997): 79–106.

Hildreth, Ronald B. *Patent Law: A Practitioner's Guide*, 3rd ed. New York: Practising Law Institute, 1998.

Hoppe, Hans-Hermann. "Fallacies of the Public Goods Theory and the Production of Security." *Journal of Libertarian Studies* 9, no. 1 (Winter 1989): 27–46.

———. *A Theory of Socialism and Capitalism*. Boston: Kluwer Academic Publishers, 1989.

———. "In Defense of Extreme Rationalism: Thoughts on Donald McCloskey's The Rhetoric of Economics." *Review of Austrian Economics* 3 (1989): 179–214.

———. *The Economics and Ethics of Private Property*. Boston: Kluwer Academic Publishers, 1993.

———. *Economic Science and the Austrian Method.* Auburn, Ala.: Ludwig von Mises Institute, 1995.

———. "The Private Production of Defense." *Journal of Libertarian Studies* 14, no. 1 (Winter 1998–1999): 27–52.

Hülsmann, Jörg Guido. "Knowledge, Judgment, and the Use of Property." *Review of Austrian Economics* 10, no. 1 (1997): 23–48.

Hume, David. *An Inquiry Concerning the Principles of Morals: With a Supplement: A Dialogue.* 1751; reprint, New York: Liberal Arts Press, 1957.

IBM. "Gallery of Obscure Patents." http://www.patents.ibm.com/gallery.

Intellectual Property Owners Association. "IPO Daily News." http://www.ipo.org.

de Jasay, Anthony. *Against Politics: On Government, Anarchy, and Order.* London: Routledge, 1997.

Jefferson, Thomas. "Letter to Isaac McPherson, Monticello, August 13, 1813." In *The Writings of Thomas Jefferson.* Vol. 8. Edited by A.A. Lipscomb and A.E. Bergh. Washington, D.C.: Thomas Jefferson Memorial Association, 1904.

Justinian. *The Institutes of Justinian: Text, Translation, and Commentary.* Translated by J.A.C. Thomas. Amsterdam: North-Holland, 1975.

Kelley, David. In "David Kelley vs. Nat Hentoff: Libel Laws: Pro and Con." Free Press Association, Liberty Audio (1987).

———. "Reply to N. Stephan Kinsella, 'Letter on Intellectual Property Rights'." *IOS Journal* 5, no. 2 (June 1995), p. 13.

Kinsella, N. Stephan. "A Civil Law to Common Law Dictionary." *Louisiana Law Review* 54 (1994): 1265–305.

———. "Letter on Intellectual Property Rights." *IOS Journal* 5, no. 2 (June 1995): 12–13.

———. "A Libertarian Theory of Punishment and Rights." *Loyola of Los Angeles Law Review* 30 (Spring 1996).

———. "New Rationalist Directions in Libertarian Rights Theory." *Journal of Libertarian Studies* 12, no. 2 (Fall 1996): 313–26.

———. "Is Intellectual Property Legitimate?" *Pennsylvania Bar Ass'n Intellectual Property Law Newsletter* 1, no. 2 (Winter 1998): 3

———. "Inalienability and Punishment: A Reply to George Smith." *Journal of Libertarian Studies* 14, no. 1 (Winter 1998–1999): 79–93.

———. "Knowledge, Calculation, Conflict, and Law: Review Essay of Randy E. Barnett, *The Structure of Liberty: Justice and The Rule of Law*." *Quarterly Journal of Austrian Economics* 2, no. 4 (Winter 1999): 49–71.

———. "A Theory of Contracts: Binding Promises, Title Transfer, and Inalienability." Paper presented at the Austrian Scholars Conference, Auburn, Ala., April 1999.

———. "In Defense of Napster and Against the Second Homesteading Rule." http://www.lewrockwell.com/orig/kinsella2.html, September 4, 2000.

Kitch, Edmund. "The Nature and Function of the Patent System." *Journal of Law and Economics* 20 (1977).

Kuester, Jeffrey. "Kuester Law: The Technology Law Resource." http://www.kuesterlaw.com.

Library of Congress. "Thomas: Legislative Information on the Internet." http://thomas.loc.gov.

Long, Roderick T. "The Libertarian Case Against Intellectual Property Rights." *Formulations* 3, no. 1 (Autumn 1995).

Machlup, Fritz. "An Economic Review of the Patent System," Study No. 15, *Subcomm. On Patents, Trademarks & Copyrights, Senate Comm. On the Judiciary*, 85th Cong., 2d Sess. (Comm. Print 1958)

Machlup, Fritz, and Edith Penrose. "The Patent Controversy in the Nineteenth Century." *Journal of Economic History* 10 (1950).

Mack, Eric. "In Defense of Blackmail." *Philosophical Studies* 41 (1982).

Mackaay, Ejan. "Economic Incentives in Markets for Information and Innovation." In "Symposium: Intellectual Property," *Harvard Journal of Law & Public Policy* 13, no. 3 (Summer 1990).

McCarthy, J. Thomas. *McCarthy on Trademarks and Unfair Competition*. 4th ed. St. Paul, Minn.: West Group, 1996.

McElroy, Wendy. "Contra Copyright." *The Voluntaryist* (June 1985).

———. "Intellectual Property: Copyright and Patent." In *The Debates of Liberty*. Edited by Wendy McElroy (forthcoming).

Meiners, Roger E., and Robert J. Staaf. "Patents, Copyrights, and Trademarks: Property or Monopoly?" In "Symposium: Intellectual Property," *Harvard Journal of Law & Public Policy* 13, no. 3 (Summer 1990).

Milgrim, Roger M. *Milgrim on Trade Secrets*. New York: Matthew Bender, 2000.

Miller, Arthur R., and Michael H. Davis. *Intellectual Property: Patents, Trademarks, and Copyrights in a Nutshell*. 2nd ed. St. Paul, Minn.: West Publishing, 1990.

Mises, Ludwig von. *The Ultimate Foundation of Economic Science: An Essay on Method*. 2nd ed. Kansas City: Sheed Andrews and McMeel, 1962.

———. *Human Action*. 3rd rev. ed. Chicago: Henry Regnery, 1966.

———. *The Theory of Money and Credit*. Translated by H.E. Batson. 1912; reprint, Indianapolis, Ind.: Liberty Fund, 1980.

———. *Epistemological Problems of Economics*. Translated by George Reisman. New York: New York University Press, 1981.

———. *Socialism: An Economic and Sociological Analysis*. 3rd rev. ed. Trans. J. Kahane. Indianapolis, Ind.: Liberty Press, 1981.

Moore, Adam D., ed. *Intellectual Property: Moral, Legal, and Ethical Dilemmas*. New York: Rowman and Littlefield, 1997.

Nance, Dale A. "Foreword: Owning Ideas." In "Symposium: Intellectual Property." *Harvard Journal of Law & Public Policy* 13, no. 3 (Summer 1990).

National Commission on New Technological Uses (CONTU) of Copyright Works. *Final Report*. July 31, 1978. Washington, D.C.: Library of Congress, 1979.

New York Intellectual Property Law Association. "FAQ on IP." http://www.nyipla.org/public/10_faq.html.

Nimmer, Melville B., and David Nimmer. *Nimmer on Copyright*. New York: Matthew Bender, 2000.

Nozick, Robert. *Anarchy, State, and Utopia*. New York: Basic Books, 1974.

Oppedahl & Larson LLP. "Intellectual Property Law Web Server." http://www.patents.com.

Palmer, Tom G. "Intellectual Property: A Non-Posnerian Law and Economics Approach." *Hamline Law Review* 12 (1989).

———. "Are Patents and Copyrights Morally Justified? The Philosophy of Property Rights and Ideal Objects." In "Symposium: Intellectual Property." *Harvard Journal of Law & Public Policy* 13, no. 3 (Summer 1990).

Patent and License Exchange. http://www.pl-x.com.

Patent and Trademark Office Society. "Home Page." http://www.ptos.org.

Patent Auction. "Online Auction for Intellectual Properties." http://www.patentauction.com.

Plant, Arnold. "The Economic Theory Concerning Patents for Inventions." In *Selected Economic Essays and Addresses*. London: Routledge & Kegan Paul, 1974.

Posner, Richard A. *Economic Analysis of Law*. 4th ed. Boston: Little, Brown, 1992.

Prusak, Leonard. "The Economic Theory Concerning Patents and Inventions." *Economica* 1 (1934): 30–51.

———. "Does the Patent System Have Measurable Economic Value?" *AIPLA Quarterly Journal* 10 (1982): 50–59.

Rand, Ayn. *Capitalism: The Unknown Ideal*. New York: New American Library, 1967.

Reisman, George. *Capitalism: A Treatise on Economics*. Ottawa, Ill.: Jameson Books, 1996.

Rothbard, Murray N. *Man, Economy, and State*. Los Angeles: Nash Publishing, 1962.

———. *An Austrian Perspective on the History of Economic Thought*. Vol. 1, *Economic Thought Before Adam Smith*. Brookfield, Vt.: Edward Elgar, 1995.

———. *The Logic of Action One*. Cheltenham, U.K.: Edward Elgar, 1997.

———. *The Ethics of Liberty*. New York: New York University Press, 1998.

Schulman, J. Neil. "Informational Property: Logorights." *Journal of Social and Biological Structures* (1990).

Source Translation Optimization. "Legal Resources and Tools for Surviving the Patenting Frenzy of the Internet, Bioinformatics, and Electronic Commerce." http://www.bustpatents.com.

Spencer, Herbert. *The Principles of Ethics.* Vol. 2. 1893; reprint, Indianapolis, Ind.: Liberty Press, 1978.

Spooner, Lysander. "The Law of Intellectual Property: or An Essay on the Right of Authors and Inventors to a Perpetual Property in Their Ideas." In *The Collected Works of Lysander Spooner.* Vol. 3. Edited by Charles Shively. 1855; reprint, Weston, Mass.: M&S Press, 1971).

Tuccille, Jerome. *It Usually Begins with Ayn Rand.* San Francisco: Cobden Press, 1971.

United States Copyright Office. http://lcweb.loc.gov/copyright.

United States Department of Commerce, Patent and Trademark Office. http://www.uspto.gov.

Universal Scientific Publications Company. http://www.tuspco.com/.

van Slyke, Paul C., and Mark M. Friedman. "Employer's Rights to Inventions and Patents of Its Officers, Directors, and Employees." *AIPLA Quarterly Journal* 18 (1990).

"Wacky Patent of the Month." http://colitz.com/site/wacky.htm.

Walker, Jesse. "Copy Catfight: How Intellectual Property Laws Stifle Popular Culture." *Reason* (March 2000).

Walterscheid, Edward C. "Thomas Jefferson and the Patent Act of 1793." *Essays in History* 40 (1998).

Woodcock, Washburn, Kurtz, Mackiewicz and Norris. "Legal Links." http://www.woodcock.com/links/links.htm.